"Packed with practical tips and helpful information, Changing Diapers is a must for the first-time cloth diaper user. Extensive tips include how to travel with cloth, how to clean cloth diapers, and what to do if you have twins. Includes clear descriptions of the types of cloth diapers and comprehensive resources on where to find them. Accessible and funny, Changing Diapers makes cloth look as easy as it really is."

—Peggy O'Mara
Editor-in-Chief, Mothering.com

"In writing Changing Diapers, Kelly Wels has drawn on her years of experience in the cloth diaper industry to create a brilliant resource for any parent interested in cloth diapering their baby. This book is a joy to read, full of "how-tos", detailed illustrations, checklists and beautiful photos. A perfectly written, helpful resource for any parent!"

—Jennifer Labit, Owner of Cotton Babies
Creator of bumGenius, Flip, and Econobum
CottonBabies.com

"Finally, a much-needed guide to the world of cloth diapering! Great for parents who don't use cloth diapers because they think it is too hard or just too gross. This book will show them how easy, affordable, beneficial, and fun cloth diapering can be."

—Sadler Merrill, Thirsties, Inc.
ThirstiesBaby.com

CHANGING DIAPERS

The HIP MOM'S GUIDE *to*
MODERN CLOTH DIAPERING

Green Team Enterprises
Waterford, Maine

The information in this book is true to the best of the author's knowledge and her ability to relate it. While the author has endeavored to present the content accurately and honestly, the author disclaims any responsibility or liability for errors, omissions, or the accuracy or reliability of the information presented. By using the information herein, you assume all risks associated with the use thereof. The author shall not in any event be liable for any direct, indirect, punitive, special, incidental, or consequential damages, including and without limitation, lost revenues or lost profits arising out of or in any way connected with the use of this material.

This book identifies product names and services known to be trademarks, registered trademarks, or service marks of their respective holders. They are used throughout this book in an editorial fashion only. In addition, terms suspected of being trademarks, registered trademarks, or service marks have been appropriately capitalized, although Kelly Wels cannot attest to the accuracy of this information. Use of a term in this book should not be regarded as affecting the validity of any trademark, registered trademark, or service mark.

VELCRO® is the name of a hook and loop fastener and is a trademark of Velcro Industries.

ISBN-13: 978-0-9835622-1-4
Library of Congress Control Number: 2011929994
Cataloging in Publication Data on file with publisher.

Green Team Enterprises
PO Box 203
Waterford, ME 04088
www.KellyWels.com

Design and production: Concierge Marketing, Inc.

Printed in the United States of America
10 9 8 7 6 5 4 3 2 1

To my amazing children:
Olivia, Hanz, and Riley

You mean the world to me.

CONTENTS

A SPECIAL THANK YOU TO THE FOLLOWING MANUFACTURERS
WHO GRACIOUSLY SENT IN THEIR PRODUCTS TO BE USED FOR
THE PHOTOS IN THIS BOOK.

www.BabyKicks.com

www.BestBottomDiapers.com

www.bumGenius.com

www.Bummis.com

www.CuteyBaby.com

www.Econobum.com

www.FlipDiapers.com

www.GoGreenPocketDiapers.com

www.HappyHeinys.com

www.HineyLineys.com

www.Kissaluvs.com

www.Knickernappies.com

www.LesliesBoutique.com

www.PlanetWiseInc.com

www.RockinGreenSoap.com

www.Rumparooz.com

www.Sustainablebabyish.com

www.ThirstiesBaby.com

www.TotsBots.com

PHOTOGRAPHY BY

Alexandra DeFurio is a professional freelance photographer. Her photos have been in *Allure* magazine, *epregnancy* magazine, and the *L.A. Times*. She lives in Santa Monica with her two daughters. (www.defuriophotography.com)

PHOTO STYLING BY

Anni Daulter is a professional cook, eco-stylist, advocate for sustainable living, and author.

Anni is the co-founder of a conscious family living magazine called *Bamboo: Conscious Family Living* and is author of *Ice Pop Joy* and *Organically Raised: Conscious Cooking for Babies & Toddlers*.

To see her eco-styling, please visit her at www.deliciousgratitude.com or visit Anni at her magazine at www.bamboofamilymag.com.

OTHER PHOTOGRAPHY BY

Chris Ruhaak at Heartland Photos & Design, www.heartlandphotos.com
Cotton Babies, Inc., www.cottonbabies.com
Jennifer Jacques, www.pinkicephotography.com
Shonta Isley, www.jmpartistry.com

CUSTOM ILLUSTRATIONS BY

Stacey Clover is the CEO/Designer at www.Icreativemedia.com. She is a loving wife and mother. Stacey is well known as one of the top designers in the youth marketing industry with a special focus on cloth diapers.

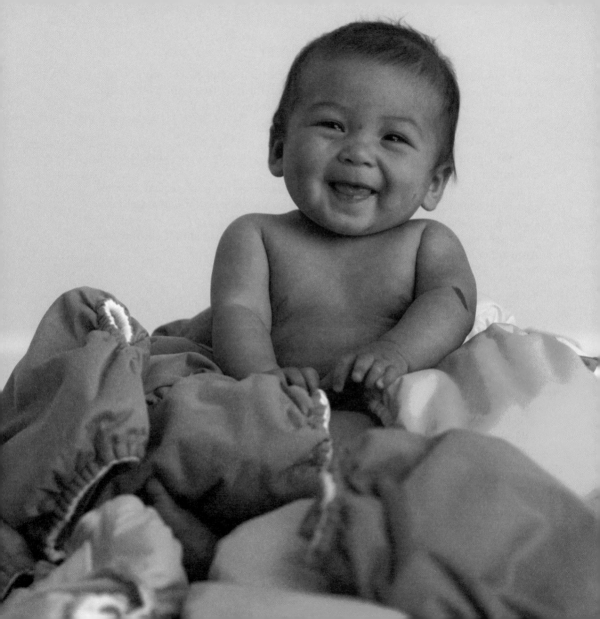

FOREWORD
HEATHER McNAMARA
Executive Director of the Real Diaper Association

The numbers are bleak: approximately 90 percent of Americans use throwaway diapers. Single-use diapers are generating 7.6 billion pounds of garbage yearly. In the two minutes it will take you to read this foreword, another 106,000 diapers will enter landfills in the U.S. This is avoidable and the book you hold in your hands can help you do your part to reduce waste while at the same time increase your baby's comfort and save money.

As Executive Director of the Real Diaper Association (RDA), the nonprofit that advocates for 100 percent reusable cloth diapers, I know well the obstacles that families face trying to use real diapers. These families need support in all forms. RDA trains and accredits local grassroots Real Diaper Circle Leaders to provide face-to-face support for thousands of cloth diaperers. Our website provides research about cloth diapers and online resources for using them.

Kelly Wels, a long-time RDA member, has been actively involved in real diaper advocacy for years. She has helped many families use and enjoy the benefits of real diapers. Now, this book provides a print resource that will hopefully reach even more "bottoms."

Choosing cloth diapers is not easy, at first. Cross-generational reusable diapering knowledge has been drowned out by Big Disposables' aggressive marketing campaigns. And many modern cloth diapers didn't even exist when your mothers were diapering. There is a learning curve. Anything that can be done to make the curve less steep is good—and this book does exactly that.

Need a primer on cloth diapering terminology? It's all covered in chapter 2. If you're looking for an economical diapering option, timeless prefolds are described on p. 62. If you need a good nighttime solution, flip to p. 135. Want to read about dads who cloth diaper? Open to chapter 8.

Choosing how to diaper a baby is among the first decisions parents make. Choosing 100 percent reusable cloth diapers sets a valuable precedent for reuse for your family, conserving precious natural and family resources and keeping environmental toxins out of your home. Let this book help you get started, and challenge yourself to creatively find the 100 percent reusable solution to any situation your family encounters.

A passionate cloth diaper movement gaining momentum. Reuse is hip again. Join us as we change diapers, one baby at a time.

Happy real diapering!

—Heather McNamara

Executive Director, Real Diaper Association

www.RealDiaperAssociation.org

THE POOP ON MODERN CLOTH DIAPERING:
AN INTRODUCTION

The modern cloth diaper choice is yours to make. If you're going to be a cloth diapering mama, you need to know the facts. And you're holding in your hands the most up-to-date, comprehensive, easy-to-read how-to book on the subject of modern cloth diapering.

*Hey, Dads! Just so you know, this book is for you too!
Please swap out "mom" for "dad" wherever appropriate.*

As a new mom, you are faced with hundreds, even thousands of decisions. This is no exaggeration either.

- Should you bank your baby's cord blood?

- Should you breastfeed, and if so, what nursing bra, breast pump, and storage bags will you use?

- Should you splurge for a designer crib or be practical and go for the $100 crib that is just as worthy?

- Should you let your baby use a binky?

- And, of course, the newest question being faced by moms today: should you use cloth diapers or disposables?

The decisions are endless and can be daunting for a new mom who is trying to figure it all out.

But if you found my book, it's likely you're taking your job as new mom decision-maker extraordinaire seriously.

The decision about diapering is a big one—after all, most parents end up changing between 5,000 and 8,000 diapers per baby. Now that's a lot of diapers!

You will change 5,000 to 8,000 diapers per baby until potty-training kicks in.

So what have you heard about cloth diapering?

For starters, the cloth diapers of today are very different from what you might be expecting.

Maybe you heard some girlfriends or moms at the gym or daycare chatting about cloth diapers and how fashionable they look and how easy they are to use. But your mom is in love with disposables because she remembers her experience with old-fashioned diapering methods.

Or maybe you are an eco-conscious mom who wants to learn about the benefits of cloth diapering and have taken it upon yourself to learn more.

Are you confused about all the information (and misinformation) floating around out there about diapering and you want to know the truth once and for all?

Spend a few minutes in an online chatroom and you get a load of information. Some moms swear by cloth, others have sworn off. You may hear buzz about one brand, only to hear a few moments later that another mom thinks the brand's quality is poor.

It seems as if every mom these days is sounding off about diapering —including the good, the bad, and the stinky.

As the depressed state of the economy butts up against the ecological green movement, more eco-friendly and cost-conscious moms tend to be looking at cloth diapers as a way to save money *and* the environment. Upon researching you will find that so-called modern cloth diapers are really hip, functional, and work just as well as, if not better than, disposables.

DON'T POO-POO IT UNTIL YOU KNOW MORE

The cloth diaper choice is yours to make. If you're going to be a cloth diapering mama, you need to know the facts. And you're holding in your hands the most comprehensive, easy-to-read, how-to book on the subject of cloth diapering.

Are you ready to "change"?

WHY LISTEN TO ME?

You may be asking yourself, *Why should I listen to you?* or *Why do I need this book?* After all, you know you can read about cloth diapering on hundreds of websites and chatrooms.

I've been an insider in the cloth diapering industry for nearly a decade. I've seen, touched, and tested just about every brand of cloth diaper imaginable—just ask my three kids. I've also documented my experiences for several years on the blog *The Cloth Diaper Whisperer* (www.theclothdiaperwhisperer.com) and on my personal blog at www.KellyWels.com—a site dedicated to educating parents about modern cloth diapering and green living.

I was the founder and owner of www.DiaperShops.com and www.KellysCloset.com, two popular online cloth diapering stores, that I later sold to spend more time on my passion as an advocate for cloth diapers.

In this book, I give you the most current, most comprehensive scoop on diapers available.

Most of all, you can take comfort in knowing that I'm a real mom, just like you! I hope that my mom-to-mom advice will show you that I know what moms need to know when making the decision to cloth diaper.

DIAPER OVERLOAD

I have researched and digested the cloth diapering information overload and decoded it into simple English. First and foremost, this book was written with an approach to keeping things simple.

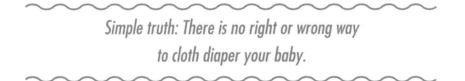

Simple truth: There is no right or wrong way to cloth diaper your baby.

As with anything in life you will find out what works best for you and your baby. Don't worry. There isn't a cloth diaper police. You will find whatever diapering system suits you and your baby (whether cloth or disposable) by experiencing diapering firsthand.

I have explored the ins and outs of cloth diapering and will share that information in an easy-to-understand, lingo-free guide. You won't find acronyms that no one understands (I don't speak in code), nor will you need to spend hours of time researching hundreds of websites and chatrooms in order to make an educated decision on what to do.

When you see a section like this, you'll find important checklists for you.

☑ This book will help you find smart answers to the following questions:

☑ Is cloth diapering right for me?

☑ What can I expect?

☑ How can I handle naysayers?

☑ How do I get started cloth diapering?

☑ What do I need to know to be successful?

☑ What resources are available to help me along the way?

In a sense, this book is everything you wanted to know about cloth diapers but were afraid to ask!

WHO IN THE WORLD CLOTH DIAPERS THEIR BABIES THESE DAYS?

Believe me, the question of who actually cloth diapers these days has crossed my mind on more than one occasion. My oldest child is a teenager now, and honestly we tried cloth diapering with her.

We weren't informed of the modern cloth diapering choices and purchased cheap department store cloth diapers. This didn't work very well, so we quickly resorted to disposables.

I found modern cloth diapers when my second child was twelve months old (as you can see, it is never too late to start!).

With my third child, not only did I use modern cloth diapers exclusively, but I had become a serious advocate for cloth diapering. I had taken it to an even higher level by opening an online modern cloth diaper store; and using every opportunity possible to encourage other moms to try it. I tested nearly every single cloth diaper made, because I insisted on trying them before I put them in my stores.

But the industry evolved again in 1999 when FuzziBunz® brand diapers came out with an innovative concept: a pocket-style cloth diaper made with fleece materials. This diaper made it easy for moms to wash diapers at home without all the complicated procedures of soaking and swirling—and they didn't require a diaper delivery service either. Since then, the major innovations keep coming, making it easy and smart to use modern cloth diapers.

Another plus? They were actually cute! That makes all the difference when we want our babies to not only feel their best, but look their best too!

Today it's hard to assess how large the cloth diapering industry really is. But consider these facts:

- Depending on sources, cloth diapers may represent a $60 million to $200 million per year industry.

- The Real Diaper Association reports that an estimated 5 to 10 percent of babies in the U.S. wear cloth diapers at least part-time. With about 16 million babies under the age of three in the U.S., this means the total cloth diaper market size is estimated between 800,000 and 1.6 million U.S. babies. It may not sound like a lot, but in a world dominated by disposable diaper ads from disposable diaper manufacturers with endless budgets, it's an amazing feat to see the little cloth diaper companies slowly become forces to be reckoned with.

- One Canadian news source pegged the sales of disposable diapers at $5.7 billion in 2008. Disposables represent 96 percent of the diapering market in North America. Happily, the cloth diaper market is rapidly growing.

Another Name for Diaper
A diaper by any other name is a nappy (or shortened form of napkin) in the United Kingdom, Ireland, and "down under" in Australia and New Zealand.

 ## Save $2,000 per Kid

A Harris Interactive survey from June 2010 sponsored by www.DiaperShops.com, reported that approximately 1 in 10 families use cloth diapers, but on the other hand, it also showed that one-third of new parents who currently use disposable diapers admit that they would switch to cloth diapers if they knew it could save them $2,000 over the course of their child's diapering years.

An info box like this gives you industry statistics.

Throughout human history, moms have struggled to contain and control the peeing and pooping until baby is fully trained to "go" in an appropriate place. In some third-world countries today, toddlers still go without a diaper or pants for obvious economic and convenience reasons.

But in developed societies, the diaper or nappy is the preferred method of keeping baby dry and the surrounding environment waste free.

JOIN THE MOVEMENT

Although we don't know for sure how many families are turning to cloth, we do know that cloth diaper sales are gaining. New cloth diaper manufacturers are emerging and thriving. In fact, according to *BabyShop* magazine in March 2010, Kanga Care, makers of the Rump•a•rooz, say they saw a 400 percent increase in gross revenue in their third year of sales.

You'll often have a nice selection of cloth diapers in your neighborhood or online retailers. But also look for them in home-based businesses where you'll usually find a helpful mom-preneur to guide you. The Resources section of this book will help you find supplies.

There's a strong marketplace for cloth diapers—one that, like your babies, will only continue to grow and grow.

As you read this book you'll see that the cloth diaper industry is probably much bigger, healthier, and more exciting and fun than you ever thought. In fact, you'll be part of a grassroots movement backed by hundreds of thousands of moms around the world who have set out to do what's right for their babies, their wallets, and their planet.

I'm always excited by the idea that a new mom is born every second. And I'm even more excited when that new mom tackles something extraordinary by embarking on a cloth diapering journey. I hope this book inspires you to get the most out of your experience and helps you relax and enjoy diapering your baby in a meaningful way.

Here's to motherhood, fluffy butts, and a learning experience ahead. Cheers!

CHAPTER 1

WHY CHOOSE CLOTH DIAPERS?

Reason #1: It's Best for Baby

Reason #2: You Can Save Big Bucks

Reason #3: You Can Be Eco-Friendly

Reason #4: Despite What You Think,
            Cloth Is Convenient

Reason #5: Yes, Cloth Diapering Is Fun
            for Many Moms

☑ What's Your Reason for Cloth Diapering?

☑ Better for baby

☑ Cheaper

☑ Environmentally friendly

☑ Convenient (yes, really!)

☑ Fun

☑ Fashionable

☑ All of the above

What might be your reason for choosing cloth diapers? With more moms flocking to cloth diapers these days, I wanted to learn about why a growing number of moms were going against the majority and choosing cloth diapers for their babies' bottoms.

After speaking with dozens of parents on this topic, let me tell you, I heard an earful.

I learned that moms cloth diaper for a variety of reasons, whether it's in the best interest of their baby's health and comfort, to save money when times are tough, or to save the environment.

Here are the facts. You decide:

REASON #1: IT'S BEST FOR BABY

I found that many moms decided to use cloth diapers because they believed it to be in the best interest of their baby's health. After doing much research on this topic, there is no clear evidence as to what is best for baby. Although a little common sense tells us otherwise. Let's talk about what we do know.

The Environmental Health Association of Nova Scotia published a *Guide to Less Toxic Products,* which includes an entire section on baby care products. The guide suggests that it's very important for parents to limit their baby's exposure to chemicals given the baby's vulnerable and developing central nervous system, which is less capable of eliminating toxins on its own.

I am no health expert, but I know that disposable diapers are made using a variety of chemicals and bleaches, potentially exposing babies to harmful chemicals around the clock.

about "Gooey gel crystals"

"My biggest reason for making the switch [to cloth diapers] was that I started finding the gooey gel crystals in my baby's diaper area. I started thinking about all the chemicals and stuff they make those disposables with and it creeped me out!" says Lisa M., a mom from Cartersville, Georgia. ●

WHAT'S INSIDE A DISPOSABLE DIAPER

Let's talk about the "stuff" inside a disposable diaper—not the stuff that eventually ends up in the diaper, but the stuff a disposable is made of.

First there's the plastic exterior that encases the inner absorbent layer and a liner. A study found that disposables release volatile chemicals including toluene (wow, that's the smelly stuff found in paints and gasoline). All are harmful with long-term exposure. I would say wearing a diaper might qualify as a long-term exposure situation.

And I might add, it takes the energy found in a cup of oil to manufacture one disposable diaper. As crude oil prices fluctuate, the cost of producing disposables could change right along with it.

Diapers in History
The first cloth diapers were soft sheets of tissue used in the sixteenth-century in England. By the nineteenth century, the homemade diaper was made of cotton and fastened with a safety pin. Cloth diapers were first manufactured in the late 1800s in the United States.

"I love knowing that
I can keep chemicals away
from my baby's bum."
—A.J., Santa Maria, California

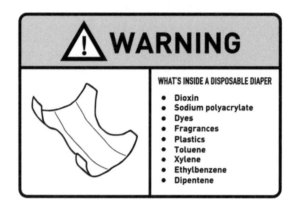

Then there's dioxin. Dioxin is one chemical prominently found in disposable diapers that has gotten the most negative press these days. Dioxin is a byproduct of the paper bleaching process commonly used in making disposable diapers. The diapers are bleached to make them look clean and white.

The Environmental Protection Agency considers dioxin to be a cancer–causing agent that can increase the risk of cancer even at low levels.

How about sodium polyacrylate? This is that crystal-like gel that helps disposable diapers absorb massive amounts of urine—some say up to eight hundred times their weight in water.

BETTER LIVING THROUGH CHEMISTRY?

Disposable diapers were introduced to the United States market in 1949, modeled perhaps from a Swedish invention made with paper inserted into rubber pants. An American mom experimented and patented her disposable design using a rubber shower curtain backing and rubber snaps.

Sodium polyacrylate was invented by scientists, . and it has been at the center of a controversial fire storm when it was removed from tampons in 1985 because of the chemical's link to toxic shock syndrome (TSS). However, in outer wear such as diapers and feminine pads where sodium polyacrylate is found, there has been no link to TSS that scientists are aware of (tampons are inserted in the body and that is believed to be the harm).

sodium polyacrylate

When moistened, sodium polyacrylate turns to gel, looks like large grains of sea salt, and often is seen on your baby's bottom between diaper changes.

Should we parents be concerned about the diaper breaking and exposing the baby directly to the substance, which could happen when the material is wet? Further, the gel is flat against the baby's skin, so it could cause irritation. The chemical is up against your baby's skin, and it could be absorbed through the skin, much like the action of birth control patches, healing creams, and nicotine patches.

Although highly unlikely, if baby somehow eats the chemical, it can cause stomach irritation as well. But it's sure a good reason to keep soiled disposable diapers away from your dog.

Another health concern related to prolonged exposure to the chemicals found in disposables is the possible links to allergies. Dyes, fragrances, plastics, toluene, xylene, ethylbenzene, dipentene, and sodium polyacrylate have all at one time been linked to allergies (and sometimes asthma).

In a 1999 study published in the *Archives of Environmental Health*, researchers found that mice exposed to the chemicals released by disposable diapers were "more likely to experience irritated airways than mice exposed to emissions from cloth diapers." In effect, the authors suggest that disposable diapers may cause "asthma-like" reactions. I'm just wondering how cute those little mice looked in the diapers in the laboratory!

Research has also indicated that lowering a baby's exposure to chemicals can benefit a baby's skin. In fact, some studies say that cloth diapering may lower a baby's incidence of diaper rash.

Fluff—a commonly used term to describe fluffy cloth diaper butts

Popular cloth diaper brands such as FuzziBunz® were invented by a mom whose baby had severe eczema that was irritated by the chemicals in disposable diapers. The daughter of the founder of Happy Heinys developed chronic lung disease, and her pediatrician suggested she use cloth diapers to aid in decreasing her daughter's need for medications and hospitalization.

about "rough, red bottoms"

"My son had severe, constant diaper rash for the first three months of his life. It was common for his bottom to bleed. He would scream every time I'd change his diaper. The doctor prescribed everything … anti-fungals and higher zinc concentrations. Finally, he said to try cloth diapers and wipes. It's hard to remember that it was for medical reasons [that we switched to cloth] because we're so addicted now! That was two years ago, and we have since had a second baby and she is in cloth too," says Brena S., a mom from Salinas, California ●

In the interest of fairness, the American Academy of Pediatrics takes no position on whether parents should use cloth or disposables. And the U.S. Consumer Product Safety Commission says it has received no significant reports of health problems or safety concerns stemming from disposable diaper usage.

Should we parents be surprised that there isn't more information easily available about the "safety" and dangers of disposable diapers? In the absence of information, parents will have to judge for themselves.

Are There Chemicals in Cloth Diapers?

Now let's tackle chemical exposure in cloth diapers. There has been no research I'm aware of on cloth diapers and their levels of chemicals, so it is hard to compare apples to apples. However, many cloth diaper brands offer organic cotton fibers that provide comfort to baby and peace of mind to moms looking to limit chemical exposure for their little ones.

No one to my knowledge has done an independent test of cloth diapers versus disposable diapers in regard to which keeps baby healthier. A few studies here and there have been funded by leading manufacturers, but, in my opinion, if disposable diapers were really so much better for baby, don't you think those companies would be churning out more studies to help keep public opinion in their favor?

But, again, that's just my opinion (and of course backed up by practical use with my own children, thousands of diaper changes, and hundreds of testimonials from moms just like you).

REASON #2: YOU CAN SAVE BIG BUCKS

Wanna save a couple thousand dollars? You can. The economics of cloth diapering can be astounding for a family on a budget.

The Bottom Line

Somebody else has figured out the real costs (and added in the energy cost of washing and drying). Cloth diapers can cost about 6 cents per diaper change, depending on which type of cloth diaper you choose. Disposables, by comparison, cost 36 cents per diaper change according to www.diaperdecisions.com.

You don't even have to do the math: a baby in cloth from birth to potty trained might cost from $381.00 compared to $2577.35 for that same baby in disposables.

While the price of cloth diapers can vary from brand to brand and style to style, it's important to understand that cloth diapering is a one-time upfront fee. Starting anywhere from $100 (for basic prefolds per baby, if you wash every other day) to $350 for designer cloth diaper brands. In comparison, disposables cost you an ongoing fee of $40 to $60 per month for all those bulky boxes you toss in your shopping cart at your favorite store.

Kids Are Expensive

Depending on where you live geographically, the costs of raising a child average about $10,000 to $11,000 a year. Multiply that by eighteen years (the time you kick them out or when their costs increase a lot because of college), that's $180,000 at minimum, and many estimates are as high as $250,000.

See for yourself by going to the calculator at the U.S. Department of Agriculture's Center for Nutrition Policy and Promotion at www. cnpp.usda.gov.

Will You Really Save Money?

The waters are a bit muddied when it comes to the actual cost savings associated with cloth diapers. That's because there are a few added costs to cloth diapering, including energy and water usage from a washing machine that runs every few days and requires hot water.

However, today's energy-efficient washers and dryers use much less water and energy than ever before. To wash most cloth diapers, no bleach is used and only a tiny speck of detergent is required (see chapter 9 on how to launder your diapers for more information).

While these costs may add up over three years, you should also consider the added costs of disposables. There will be many times when you make a run to the store simply to buy diapers (after all, you ran out and baby needs a diaper and it's midnight, quick!).

Do you factor in gas money (and the fact that you'll probably spend more at the store than you planned with all these unexpected trips)? At some point these minor costs are a "wash."

What Moms Say... about "fluffy bums"

"Cloth diapering sounded cheaper to do when I was first considering it, but the initial cost was a bit daunting because I didn't know if I would stick with it. One day I found a killer deal on a large lot of used FuzziBunz® and so it was a go. I will admit that I loved looking at them all fluffy and ready to be used once our little bun arrived. The switch from the first few days of disposables to cloth was easy enough, and I loved patting my baby on her huge fluffy bum!" says Berkeley Y., mom from Durham, North Carolina ●

If parents have multiple children, they can reuse the cloth diapers for a second time, saving even more and maximizing the few hundred they spent upfront on a cloth diapering system:

$350 vs. $2,400 x 2 kids.

That's real money and real savings with cloth.

Do the Math

The DiaperPin.com has a calculator to help you determine the cost of using cloth vs. disposables: www.diaperpin.com.

What Moms Say... **about "totally saving money"**

"I think we totally save money by using cloth. My water bill only went up $3 a month, and I estimated that I was spending $40 a month on disposables before. I have spent maybe $300 on diapers and inserts and have cloth diapered for four months so far. The diapers I have are in excellent condition, and I foresee them lasting all through my son's diapering years and possibly being in good enough condition for the next child too," says Georgia mom, Lisa M. ●

REASON #3: YOU CAN BE ECO-FRIENDLY

While the costs of disposable diapering can weigh on a family's wallet, our precious planet Earth might pay far greater "costs."

In doing research for this book, I noticed a lot of companies and studies trying to diminish the environmental aspects of cloth diapering. These detractors say we waste water by washing diapers, which has similar detrimental impacts on the environment as the manufacturing of disposable diapers. But logic tells me otherwise.

If buying single-use items were truly better for the environment, why do we wash our clothes or dishes after each use? Isn't it cheaper to just manufacture these products over and over again?

What Moms Say... about "washing versus tossing"

"I don't believe for one second that the water I use to wash them [cloth diapers] is worse than throwing them in the landfill," says Edna C., a mom from New York. ●

The way I see it, there are many more "costs" than meet the eye with manufacturing disposable diapers.

- It's not just the use of raw materials (over and over and over again), but it's shipping those raw materials to the diaper manufacturing plants.

- It's the tools and energy required over and over again to make disposable diapers.

- It's the packaging waste created time and time again.

- It's transportation gas and waste and all the energy used to keep the lights on at the corporate offices of these big diaper-making conglomerates.

Further, let's not forget the resources required to haul our 3.5 million tons of dirty diapers or 28 billion disposables trucked to landfills each year and the energy required to make those little neatly wrapped stink bombs disappear (outta sight, outta mind, right?). Not for hundreds of years.

Disposables diapers are just resource-intensive from start to finish no matter how big companies try to spin it.

I didn't set out to write this book to prove that cloth diapering was more environmentally friendly (I'll let the experts do that), but I can tell you to read between the lines of anything you read.

The companies that manufacture disposable diapers have a lot of money at stake (billions and billions), so it seems you can fund a study to "prove" anything these days to distort the truth or detract from the real issues at stake.

On the other end of the spectrum, many cloth diaper manufacturers were started by women entrepreneurs who have organically grown their businesses over time—not mega-corporations. That might be why we don't see a lot of multi-million-dollar studies pitting cloth against disposables—these mom-preneurs are concentrating on growing their businesses, not proving their product is superior.

Bottom line: Cloth diapers today are nothing like diapers you may have worn as a baby and are less environmentally resource-intensive than ever before.

In other words, please read everything you see or hear about the downside of cloth diapers with a grain of salt and a dose of healthy skepticism.

Bear in mind that many of the studies on disposables versus cloth diapers are outdated and didn't take into account modern cloth diapers and modern energy-efficient washers used to wash them. In the olden days (ask your mother and granny), cloth diapers were bleached and required an intensive amount of resources to wash and dry or have picked up and delivered each week.

"Cloth diapering makes me feel empowered, earthy, crunchy, loving, frugal, happy, healthy, smart and AMAZING!"

—H.F., Dunkirk, Indiana

More Eco-Friendly Tips

If you want to make your cloth diapering experience as eco-friendly as possible, consider doing the following:

When you see a section like this, you'll find important eco-friendly tips.

- Buy enough diapers so you only have to wash every three to four days versus daily. This will ensure you wash larger loads and use less water and energy each week. Plus your diapers will last longer with less wear and tear!

- Only use energy-efficient washers and dryers (A+ ratings preferred). You'll save on energy and water costs, so it pays off in the long run.

- Use cold water to pre-wash your diapers and only use hot water for one cycle. Just don't make the water too hot. It can break down the waterproof barrier on some diapers.

- Air dry your diapers when possible, especially on sunny days when you can lay them out in the sun or pin them up on a clothesline. The sun can help get rid of stains and dry your diapers with no energy waste.

❀ Don't ever throw away your diapers. Use them for multiple children and then resell them online or donate them to a charity. Some diapers come with elastic, Velcro-style, or snap replacement kits so you can fix any wear or tear issues and preserve your diapers for a long, long time.

❀ Use clean and eco-friendly detergents when washing diapers. You won't need harmful bleaches when cleaning modern cloth diapers.

Trash Talk

It's no secret that disposable diapers contribute to the millions of tons of untreated sewage that go to landfills each year. Such sewage is a cause for concern for many people due to the possibilities of ground water contamination.

A spokesperson from the EPA (Environmental Protection Agency) told WebMD that the agency didn't consider diapers a threat to ground water since modern U.S. landfills are engineered to protect the environment from contaminants.

That may put some moms' minds at ease, but my motto is to prevent the sewage from getting into the landfills in the first place. Safe or not, would you buy a home next to a landfill? I thought not.

Time magazine reports that 27.4 billion disposable diapers are used each year in the United States alone, and, according to EPA estimates, that translates into nearly 4 million tons of waste going into landfills.

This Is Not Degrading

Depending on the source, experts estimate that disposable diapers may still be stinking up landfills for generations to come—possibly up to 500 years. Consider that the disposable diaper you remove from your baby today may remain in the environment when that baby is a great great grandfather and even longer. So as babies fill up their diapers, landfills are filling up with tons of chemical-laden nonbiodegradable substances—those 6,000 disposable diapers you use before baby learns to say, "Potty."

Water contamination and trash are another story in third-world countries where there are no modern sewage systems and no curb-side trash pickup. These countries use cloth diapers they can wash at home. If they didn't, piles of disposable diapers filled with human feces would riddle the streets and create more harm than good.

What Moms Say... about "diapers in third-world countries"

Disposable diapers are commonplace in developed countries, but in under-developed countries throughout parts of South America, the Middle East, and Africa, no garbage truck comes by once a week!

So it's no wonder that in third-world countries, cloth diapers are the accepted norm. There is nowhere to dispose of disposable diapers so they would become more of a burden than a welcome convenience.

When New York mom Edna C. adopted seven-month-old baby Makensie from Ethiopia, she found that the orphanage Makensie lived in exclusively used cloth diapers.

"When I first visited Makensie, the orphanage was using mainly prefolds. When I went back for a second visit, I brought about thirty pocket diapers to leave behind so I could make diapering easier for them," says Edna. "They don't have washing machines, so everything they clean is washed by hand. They also don't have a trash system. In some ways they have it more right than we do."

Edna says she didn't even think of bringing disposables with her when she went back and forth to Ethiopia. The women at the orphanage helped her wash her diapers.

"I used the flip diaper when traveling internationally because they are compact to fit in luggage and they are flat so they dry more quickly," she says, adding that pocket diapers can be bulky to pack and therefore expensive when you consider having to pay for extra baggage. ●

Mother Earth Pays the Final Cost

I will leave you with one final thought on the environmental impact of disposable diapers:

Consider all costs on Mother Earth, from cradle to grave, as the illustration shows. Making disposable diapers involves so much more than cutting down trees. It requires transportation, ink for printing packaging, gas emissions for hauling natural resources and end products to stores, to your home, and eventually to the landfill.

"cloth diapering feels like I'm making a positive impact on my child's well-being and his environment."

—A.K., Richmond, Virginia

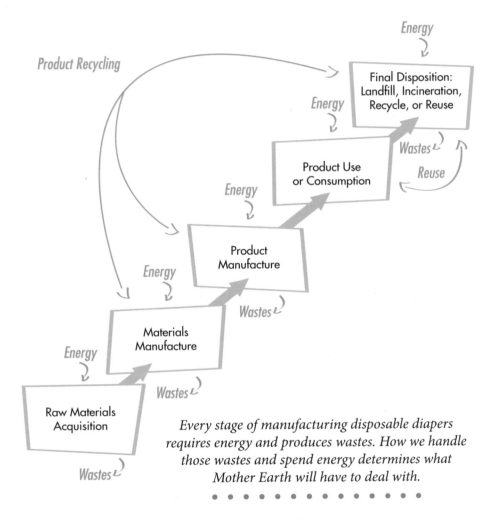

Energy

Final Disposition:
Landfill, Incineration,
Recycle, or Reuse

Product Recycling

Energy

Wastes

Reuse

Product Use
or Consumption

Energy

Product
Manufacture

Energy

Wastes

Materials
Manufacture

Energy

Wastes

Raw Materials
Acquisition

Wastes

Every stage of manufacturing disposable diapers requires energy and produces wastes. How we handle those wastes and spend energy determines what Mother Earth will have to deal with.

REASON #4: DESPITE WHAT YOU THINK, CLOTH IS CONVENIENT

As silly as it sounds to some parents, cloth diapering really can be a convenient diapering option.

Imagine not having to run to the store every time you need more diapers. Imagine never having to lug a heavy box of diapers home and then finding a place to store them each and every time.

Instead, with cloth diapers you simply put in a load of laundry at night and have clean diapers in the morning.

What Moms Say... about "never having to buy disposables"

"I love that I never have to run to the store to buy disposables. Worst case scenario is I have to do a load of laundry. The good news is I don't have to go anywhere or buy anything … ever!" says Edna C. ●

REASON #5: YES, CLOTH DIAPERING IS FUN FOR MANY MOMS

Many women I talked to told me they love cloth diapering, and some are even addicted to it! They love the fashion-forward colorful diapers and talking about cloth diapering with other moms. Join the online blogs and have your say (see the Resources section for websites).

What Moms Say... **about "the secret club"**

"The only moms I know who love diapers and can talk about them endlessly are those who cloth diaper. That's one of the big perks of cloth diapering: It makes something that most parents dread somewhat fun," says Berkeley Y. ●

"I think the best part is the camaraderie that you feel with other cloth diapering moms. It's like you are in a secret club that promotes healthy things for both your children and the planet!" says Lisa M. ●

CHAPTER 2

SNAPPIS, DOUBLERS, AIOs, AND POCKETS:
UNDERSTANDING BASIC CLOTH DIAPER TALK

It's a whole new world and a brand new language. You've got to talk the talk before you can enter the cloth diaper fold.

Today's cloth diapering world is filled with a maze of terms that can be quite confusing and even downright frightening to a new mom who simply wants to know how to cloth diaper her baby.

Once you decide to cloth diaper (or at least try it), you will want to decide on a style, brand, and the works.

Let's talk about the basics. The best piece of advice I can give when you are first starting out on your cloth diapering journey is twofold:

1. Be sure to sample three or four different brands and styles of diapers before making a large purchase. Every diaper fits every baby differently (as with any clothing product), and you don't want to get stuck with one brand when your baby does better with another.

2. If you have never cloth diapered before, I highly recommend starting out with all-in-ones (AIOs) or pocket-style diapers. These diapers are the easiest to use and are most like disposables. The goal is to get you to enjoy using cloth diapers rather than to complicate the process.

What Moms Say... about "the overwhelming choices"

"I did a lot of research on cloth diapering online while I was pregnant. I was completely overwhelmed by all the choices (and the hormones!), and decided against it. After a friend of mine from college had her baby, I asked her about cloth diapering, and she assured me that the laundry wasn't that bad. Once I dug into the research again, I don't know how, but I quickly settled on pockets (though I tried prefolds and covers at first ... not for me!). I've been a cloth diaperer since!" says Lisa M. ●

New moms will be asked if they're using all-in-ones (AIOs) or pockets, prefolds or fitteds, snaps or Velcro-like fasteners, and hemp or cotton. The decisions are vast for any cloth diapering newbie.

Let's go through some of the terminology you'll need to know if you're going to be a cloth diapering mama—just the basics, of course!

CLOTH DIAPERING 101

When considering the various cloth diaper brands, you will see that you have a lot to choose from. So let's discuss some of the most common cloth diapering options that you should become familiar with. The pages that follow illustrate the different types of cloth diapers and their accessories.

 ## ALL-IN-ONE CLOTH DIAPERS

All-in-One Cloth Diapers are commonly referred to as AIOs and pronounced *aye-eye-oh*. AIO diapers are the closest diapers to a disposable because they fit on your baby like a disposable. The absorbency layer is sewn into the diaper (so they can be quite thick, which makes drying times longer), but AIOs don't require "stuffing" the diaper with an absorbent layer like a pocket requires. This may make it a bit more convenient than pocket diapers.

I call these diapers the "Daddy and Daycare Friendly" diapers!

ALL-IN-ONE CLOTH DIAPERS

The closest cloth diaper to a disposable.

STEP 1

Slide open diaper under baby and pull up front.

STEP 2

Fasten sides to front of the diaper.

Examples of an "AIO" diaper include the bumGenius® Elemental Organic All-in-One, bumGenius Sized All-in-One, and GroVia One-Size All-in-One.

• •

www.KellyWels.com

POCKET CLOTH DIAPERS

Pocket Cloth Diapers are commonly referred to simply as "pockets." Pocket diapers have three layers:

1. An outer, waterproof shell,

2. An attached inner layer (typically made of fleece), and

3. A pocket opening where you stuff it with absorbent layers, known as the insert.

The benefit to the pocket style is that you can take out the insert and wash and dry the diaper more efficiently than if it were all sewn together like an AIO.

Fluffy Stuff!

Is diapering different for boys and girls? Boys usually need more absorbency in the front and girls in the middle. If you are using pocket-style diapers, you can customize and position the inserts up higher for boys or more in the middle for girls to maximize the absorbency of the diaper.

POCKET CLOTH DIAPERS

STEP 1

Put insert inside of the pocket.

STEP 2

Slide diaper under baby and pull up front around baby's belly.

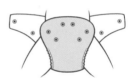

STEP 3

Fasten sides to front of the diaper.

Examples of pocket diapers include FuzziBunz Perfect Size, bumGenius, BabyKicks, and Happy Heinys brand diapers.

• •

ONE-SIZE CLOTH DIAPERS

One-Size Cloth Diapers typically fit a baby from birth to potty training (about 7.5 pounds through 35 pounds). Many of the pocket brands come in regular-sized and one-sized diapers. The benefit of a one-size diaper is that it can be used longer and sized accordingly with snaps or adjustable elastic as baby grows. But many families with larger or smaller babies will likely enjoy the "sized" diapers better.

Fluffy Stuff!

Try out several brands before you buy a whole stock of one-size diapers. Different brands have their own fit, sizing-techniques and features.

 ONE-SIZE CLOTH DIAPERS

Most one-size cloth diapers have a snap down "rise" that allows you to adjust the diaper from newborn to a potty training toddler.

STEP 1

For newborn setting snap top row of snaps to bottom rows of snaps so no snaps will show.

STEP 2

For infant setting have one row of snaps exposed (depending on the brand).

STEP 3

For toddler setting un-snap all rows of snaps (depending on the brand).

Examples of one-size diapers include bumGenius, FuzziBunz One-Size, Rump•a•rooz, and itti bitti brand diapers.

• •

 ALL-IN-TWO CLOTH DIAPERS

All-in-Two Cloth Diapers—we call these AI2 or *aye-eye-twos*. AI2 diapers feature the benefits of an AIO and a pocket diaper in one. The diaper has removable inserts, much like a pocket diaper, but the inserts typically lie on top of the diaper or snap into place on top of the diaper. There is no "stuffing" of an insert required.

> ## 🌱 Fluffy Stuff!
>
> Yikes, you ran out of inserts, and the washer load is in the dryer. If you run out of inserts, you can use any material (like a dishtowel or wash cloth) as a substitute.

 ALL-IN-TWO CLOTH DIAPERS

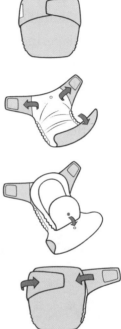

STEP 1

Open diaper.

STEP 2

Lay in insert (or snap in insert depending on the brand).

STEP 3

Slide diaper under baby and fasten sides to front of the diaper.

Examples of an AI2 diaper include Amp and the GroVia diaper systems.

• •

FLAT CLOTH DIAPERS

Flat Cloth Diapers (let's just call 'em flats) are the most basic of cloth diapering options. They are simply large squares of a single layer of fabric (usually 27 x 27 inches) that must be folded in order to fit the baby (you fold it so that the thickness of the fabric is in the center where your baby urinates). You can either fasten the diaper onto the baby with a pin or simply fold the diaper and stuff it inside a diaper cover.

🌱 Fluffy Stuff!

These diapers are handy for all types of baby needs, so have a couple on hand.

FLAT CLOTH DIAPERS

STEP 1

Fold diaper in half.

STEP 2

Bring the top corner over and pull it over to the right.

STEP 3

Turn the entire diaper over.

STEP 4

Fold the diaper in the vertical part.

STEP 5

The diaper is ready to place on baby. Fasten with Snappi Diaper Faster (page 70) or pins.

Examples of a flat include the OsoCozy Birdseye Cotton Flat Cloth Diapers.

• •

PREFOLD CLOTH DIAPERS

Prefold Cloth Diapers (commonly shortened to prefolds) are one step up from flats because they are flat sheets of fabric but have thicker layers of fabric sewn in the middle where baby requires the most absorbency. They too must be fastened with a pin or simply stuffed inside a diaper cover.

Fluffy Stuff!

Once your kids are potty trained, smart moms and dads find useful ways to use prefolds. Use them as household cleaning cloths and polishing rags. And they're great for washing and drying cars.

PREFOLD CLOTH DIAPERS

STEP 1

Lay prefold diaper flat.

STEP 2

Fold the bottom of the diaper up 3".

fold

STEP 3

Fold the left panel across the middle panel of the diaper to create a pocket.

fold

pocket

STEP 4

Fold the right panel inside, and tuck into the pocket you created in step 3.

fold

pocket

STEP 5

Open out the top corners formed by the left and right sections that overlap. Place baby in the center, pull up the bottom, and pin the corners over the baby (or use Snappi Diaper Fastener).

Prefolds can be found at most major baby products retail stores. Many moms use prefolds as burp cloths rather than as diapers.

• •

FITTED (OR CONTOURED) CLOTH DIAPERS

Fitted (or Contoured) Cloth Diapers (referred to as fitteds) provide a contoured fit because they are elasticized in the legs and waist and have either snap or Velcro-like closures. They require a separate diaper cover to contain wetness.

Fitted diapers require a diaper cover. Simply slide a fitted diaper under baby and fasten diaper. Then slide a diaper cover under baby and over the fitted diaper and fasten.

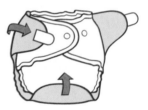

Example of a fitted includes the BabyKicks One-Size Hemp Fitted Diaper, Sloomb Fitted Cloth Diapers and the Kissaluvs Fitted Cloth Diapers.

• •

🌸 Fluffy Stuff!

Laundry Tabs are a nifty feature in some diapers. They are VELCRO-brand fasteners or some sort of hook-and-loop type fastener. Laundry tabs are there to protect your cloth diaper investment from wear and tear in the wash. Before washing the diaper, you need to fold down the Velcro-style tab so the hook side isn't exposed in the wash—otherwise it will snag other diapers in the wash (wash diapers without other clothing in the load).

HYBRID DIAPERS

Hybrid diapers aren't quite a cloth diaper and aren't quite disposable diapers either. Rather, this is where cloth and disposables meet! These diapers typically have a cloth outer shell that is washable and reusable, but the inside is usually flushable or disposable.

These systems are typically the most pricey, but some moms are willing to pay more for the opportunity to flush or decompose their diaper on the spot. These are great go-to diapers when cloth isn't practical and a disposable product is necessary (for travel). The good news is many hybrid systems accommodate both a disposable and reusable cloth insert.

 HYBRID DIAPERS

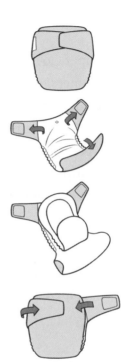

STEP 1

Open diaper.

STEP 2

*Lay cloth or disposable insert
in the center.*

STEP 3

*Slide diaper under baby and fasten
sides to front of the diaper.*

Examples of hybrid diapers include gDiapers, Flip, and GroVia.

• •

 DIAPER COVERS

Diaper Covers are used as the outer waterproof layer that fits over flat diapers, prefolds, and fitted diapers. Diaper covers (sometimes called diaper wraps) come in a variety of options such as wool, fleece, and PUL (polyurethane laminate). Some AIOs and AI2s also require a diaper cover, which depends on whether there is one attached.

Most pocket diapers have a waterproof outer shell attached to it and do not require a separate diaper cover.

Diaper covers come in a variety of fabric options and can fasten with snaps or Velcro.

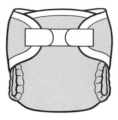

Examples of diaper covers include the Thirsties Duo Diaper Wrap, Bummis Super Whisper Wrap, and Kissaluvs Wool Soaker.

· ·

"I like that my kids' poop
won't be preserved for 500 years
in a landfill. That's not a legacy
I think they would like!"

—V.C., Plattsburg, New York

DIAPER ACCESSORIES

Snappi

A Snappi is the brand name of a commonly used tool that holds a basic cloth diaper together instead of a pin. Most modern cloth diapers use snaps or Velcro-style hooks and loops to fasten the diaper on the baby, but prefolds and even some fitted or contoured diapers do not have a fastener. The Snappi is triangular in shape and has grippers that hold the diaper to the baby without having to use a diaper pin.

Photo by: Shonta Isley

This is what a real baby looks like when wearing a Snappi

• • • • • • • • • • • • • • • • • •

SNAPPI

STEP 1

Stretch Snappi in all directions.
(Work it, girl!)

STEP 2

Hook right.

STEP 3

Hook left.

STEP 4

Pull down and hook center.

STEP 5

Cover diaper and Snappi
with a diaper cover.

INSERTS, DOUBLERS AND LINERS

Inserts (Sometimes called "soakers")

Inserts aren't a cloth diapering type, per se, however inserts are needed for any pocket diapering system and provide the layers of absorbency needed to allow a pocket diaper to function properly. Some parents make their own inserts by stuffing flats, prefolds, or even washcloths inside the pocket opening, but others use high-tech inserts made of micro-terry cotton or hemp, which are quite absorbent.

Doublers

Doublers are thick pads that you can use for extra absorbency in your cloth diapers. Simply add the rectangular-shaped pads on top of any cloth diaper for extra leak protection—great for heavy wetters or nighttime use.

Liners

Liners are usually thin, rectangular-shaped pads that go between your baby's bottom and the diaper. Many parents use them so poop is easier to clean up. Some liners are reusable/washable, while others are flushable or disposable. Some moms use plain, flat diapers as a liner to save money. Liners can also be helpful if you need to put a diaper ointment on your baby. You don't want to put the ointment directly on the diaper because it could ruin it.

Inserts, doublers and liners come in all different shapes, sizes, fabrics, and absorbencies to make sure your baby is always dry and comfortable.

United States vs. Overseas Manufacturing

If you spend any amount of time online, you'll see that a debate rages on about which are better: cloth diapers manufactured in the United States or those made overseas.

What this debate comes down to is your personal choice. If you only drive U.S.-made cars and buy U.S.-manufactured products and that is important to your family, then the choice is clear to stick with a U.S.-made cloth diaper. In other words, if everything you bought for your baby and your house is "made in the U.S.A.," then obviously this is something you worry about in terms of your diapers.

On the other hand, if you have no idea where your crib, stroller, and bouncy seat were manufactured, chances are you can be open-minded to any cloth diaper, regardless of where it's manufactured.

If you're feeling stuck in the middle on this issue, a good way to feel better about your purchase is to understand the working conditions overseas. Do employees get fair wages and proper benefits? I think you'll find that the answers are overwhelmingly "yes!"

Also, just remember that you're a mom. You have a lot to worry about. Do what's right for you and your family.

WHAT YOU NEED TO KNOW
ABOUT CLOTH DIAPER FABRICS

The world of cloth diapering employs a variety of fabrics:

- Synthetic fabrics are excellent at keeping your baby dry.

- Organic fabrics aren't treated with chemicals and are just as functional.

Let's discuss some of the basic fabrics used in cloth diapers and how they work.

Bamboo: Bamboo is super soft and almost has a luxury feel to it. The natural fabric is known for its breathability and absorbency. Bamboo Baby and Bamboozle are brands that are dedicated to using bamboo fabrics.

Many experts say that bamboo is an eco-friendly choice because bamboo grows fast and is considered an endlessly renewable resource. It also doesn't involve any insecticides to grow, unlike cotton, although there is some controversy over the way bamboo is produced, so you want to do your research before committing.

Cotton: Cotton has gotten a bad rap in the cloth diaper world because cotton production typically requires pesticides to grow and residue may remain on the cloth itself. Cotton also goes through a bleaching process that can be harmful to the eco-system as well. That said, cotton is still one of the softest, most comfortable and breathable of all fibers, making it a good choice for cloth diapers and good for baby's bottom.

Organic Cotton: Organic cotton feels the same as conventional cotton, but it is grown in a way that makes a low impact on the environment—no pesticides and fertilizers and no genetically engineered seed for organic farming. In fact, certified organic cotton is grown in fields where pesticides have not been used for at least three years.

PUL: PUL stands for polyurethane laminated fabric, which is fabric that is layered with a waterproof backing. It's durable and reliable. That's why it's used in so many cloth diapers these days. PUL is necessary to keep wetness contained within the diaper. The downside to PUL is that it's not biodegradable. Many experts say it is very functional, so even though it doesn't biodegrade in a landfill when it is eventually worn and tossed away, it is used for a long time and rarely will need to end up in the landfill.

Wool: Wool is a common fabric used as the waterproof barrier in a diaper. Heck, wool keeps sheep dry and makes us some warm and comfy sweaters, it'll surely keep your baby warm and dry as well. Wool comes, of course, from the coat of a sheep or lamb and is considered a natural fiber (as opposed to man-made fibers such as polyester).

Many cloth diaper companies use wool for diaper covers because wool can repel water. Although wool can be a good option, it does require some extra care when washing (see washing details in chapter 9). Plus, the fibers tend to stiffen when they dry out so you have to use care when laundering them.

Hemp: Hemp is a very durable fabric (it's three to four times stronger than cotton) and is known for its ultra-absorbency and anti-microbial qualities (it has been suggested that hemp may protect your baby from fungus and bacteria).

Hemp is considered eco-friendly because pesticides are not needed to farm hemp. It is also porous so it can help your baby's bottom "breathe," and it keeps your baby's bottom cool in the summer and warm in the winter. Hemp is only found in its natural color, so it's not as cute as some of the cotton designs. But if "cuteness" isn't of concern to you, then hemp is a good choice.

Diapering Products Made with Hemp

- BabyKicks Hemparoo Joey Bunz (made of 45% certified organic cotton and 55% natural hemp)
- Knickernappies Super-Do Hemp Terry Inserts (contains six layers of hemp terry and two layers of microfiber)
- Baby Beehinds One Size Hemp Fitted Diaper (made from 55% hemp and 45% certified organic cotton)
- FuzziBunz Hemp Diapers with a hemp cloth insert
- Happy Hempys One-Size Hemp Fitted Diaper

> 🌿 Fluffy Stuff!
>
> Before using your hemp diaper or insert, wash it six to eight times in hot water using a cloth diaper–approved detergent. Dry the product between wash cycles. This process will remove most natural oils from the product and make it more absorbent.

Micro-terry: Micro-terry is a polyester blend material that is super thirsty and absorbent without all the bulk of cotton. Many pocket diapers come with a micro-terry insert to absorb baby's urine. Micro-terry washes easily, although it does stain. Micro-terry inserts typically come in rectangular- and contour-shaped styles.

> 🌿 Fluffy Stuff!
>
> Never put a micro-terry cloth directly next to baby's skin. It's so absorbent that it will pull out the skin's natural oils, which can lead to chafing and irritation.

Polar Fleece: FuzziBunz was the first diaper manufacturer to use fleece. Its founder discovered that fleece wicks away moisture from the skin to allow urine to pass through the fleece, keeping your baby's bottom dry. Fleece is a synthetic material, which some cloth diaper users frown upon. However, it is super effective and soft and keeps baby dry, so the fabric definitely has its pros.

Sherpa Terry: Sherpa Terry is the fabric you find in linens and towels. It's basically a knit terry that is brushed so it has raised fibers. It is comprised of a cotton-polyester blend and is commonly used in cloth diapers.

In summary, the key point to remember when making choices about cloth diapers is to keep things simple. Sample different brands and styles.

Decide first if you want to choose a completely natural/organic fabric. If this is your choice, then a more traditional choice of prefold-style cloth diapers would be suited to your needs. If the fabric selection is not a top factor, then I would recommend trying an AIO and pocket-style diaper and purchase a few types of inserts with different fabric choices.

C — Chemical Free!

L — Leakproof

O — One Size

T — Tender

H — Handy

D — Dependable

I — Ideal

A — Adorable

P — Penny Pinching

E — Eco-friendly

R — Rash-free

—*A.C. Wantage, New Jersey*

CHAPTER 3

BRANDS, DEBATES, AND DATES:

GETTING STARTED WITH CLOTH

If you've decided cloth diapering is right for your family, then figuring out what brand to buy will be your next big step. It's like standing at the entrance of an amusement park. You see all the attractions, but figuring out where to start can be difficult. You have to start somewhere. Let's talk about your options.

DIAPER LIKE A PRO

Wondering what supplies you need to be cloth diapering like a pro? Wonder no more! Use this easy-to-follow checklist (used with permission from *www.DiaperShops.com*) to help you make sure you buy all the supplies you need and nothing more.

☑ **Diapers:** You'll need at least twelve if you plan on doing laundry daily, or twenty to twenty-five if you plan to do laundry every other day. When deciding what type of diaper (all-in-ones, pockets, etc.) and brands, make sure to give each a try first and see what works best for you. Some babies and moms do better with one type or brand over another. Try before you buy.

☑ **Wipes:** Reusable wipes are a great option to make your cloth diapering experience ultra-green. Keep twenty-five to fifty wipes on hand depending on how often you do laundry. You'll also want to keep a small container of water near your changing area for wetting wipes before use. If you don't use reusable wipes, make sure you have a stash of disposable wipes and a trash can by your changing table.

☑ **Large Diaper Pail:** You'll want a reusable diaper pail to store dirty diapers between washes. Some diaper pails can hang on a hook or doorknob, while others line a trashcan. Some even zip open at the bottom to allow easy unloading of dirty diapers into the wash. You wash your diaper pail along with your diapers.

☑ **Small Diaper Wet Tote:** You'll want to purchase one to three diaper totes for storing dirty diapers while on the road. These are small, tote-sized bags that generally have a snap or zipper closure at the top to keep dirty diapers contained until you get home to wash them. Simply store them in your diaper bag or stroller until you get home. Diaper totes are washed along with your dirty diaper wash.

☑ **Extra Inserts:** If you use pocket diapers and have a heavy wetter, you'll want to keep some extra micro-terry or hemp inserts on hand. Use two inserts inside your pocket diaper at night to ensure a leak-free night.

☑ **Diaper Sprayer:** The diaper sprayer is one of the best investments a cloth diapering mama can make. The sprayer easily attaches to your toilet to enable you to rinse off ultra-poopy diapers over your toilet, not in your washing machine.

☑ **Detergent:** You'll want to make sure you have manufacturer-approved detergent on hand for washing your cloth diapers. Most cloth diapers are made with fleece fabric that repels liquid if soap scum is present. You'll want to use clean rinsing formulas such as Rockin' Green Cloth Diaper Detergent, Vaska, or Allen's Naturally.

☑ **Clothesline:** This is optional, but many moms enjoy hanging their cloth diapers to dry to save energy. Use the clothesline inside during the winter, and outside in the summer for fresh-smelling diapers.

☑ **Patience:** Learning cloth diapering takes time, patience, and commitment. You may have some challenges at first, but stick with it and it will become second nature in no time.

CHOOSING THE RIGHT BRAND FOR YOU AND YOUR BABY

In the last few years, the cloth diapering industry has exploded and there are so many brands that it's difficult to keep up. As someone who has been an insider in the cloth diapering industry for nearly a decade, and as the mother of an infant myself, I can say that I've been in the fortunate situation to try just about every cloth diaper imaginable.

I do not recommend one brand over the other, but I do feel each has its distinct advantages (and disadvantages), which I will make you aware of. At the end of the day (and in the middle of the night), you know that every mom and baby is different. What works for one family doesn't always work for another.

Follow these general guidelines when making a decision about which brand to purchase:

Learn about a few brands. If you attempt to learn about all the brands, you will get lost. I recommend that you narrow your search to three to four brands that fall within the "type" (pocket, AIO, AI2, and other types) that you're interested in. Just be careful not to let overzealous review sites taint your decision. Rather, look at the websites of each brand, talk to trusted sources you know, and test drive a diaper for a day and see what you think. I also recommend sampling the brands that you narrowed down before you purchase a large quantity of one brand.

Talk to friends. You may not have a friend who uses cloth, but chances are there is a support group for cloth diapering moms in your area. Moms who use cloth diapers are usually more than willing to share their experiences with a newbie, so start asking away! The online community is a great resource for asking questions; however, some people have ulterior motives online so trust your instincts and do your homework before making any firm choices. See the listing of mommy blogs on cloth diapering in the Resources section. Listen in on their discussions.

Sample a few brands. Don't buy one brand of cloth diaper just because you heard it was good. Instead, try your friend's diapers or order a sampling of several diapers online. Try them on your baby before washing to see if they fit well. Sample one diaper before ordering your entire stash. Most retailers don't let you return your diapers if they are worn or washed, so don't waste hundreds of dollars on a single brand only to find out later they don't work for you.

If you don't like a certain brand you bought, try selling or swapping it online at www.DiaperSwappers.com. Any unused diapers can typically be returned for a full refund (make sure you work with a retailer with an open return policy). Some online stores offer guarantees that you'll like their cloth diapers or your money back, which can feel like a safer bet for you. If you have a diaper you bought but didn't really use, then try to sell it or swap it online. There is a thriving online marketplace for used cloth diapers (even your local www.Craigslist.com).

Stick with it. Some moms may have a difficult first experience with a cloth diaper, but after they and their babies get the hang of things, it ends up working out just fine. Don't judge your entire experience based on one day of cloth diapering. Stick with it and give it the old college try. The first time I cloth diapered my baby he had massive diarrhea. I was determined not to let a few messy diapers get in the way of what could be a good thing for my family. I was, of course, right!

See for yourself. You may hear a bad thing about a brand of diaper and then try the brand for yourself and love it. Always try to see for yourself what the good and bad attributes might be in a diaper. It's worth repeating this sentiment I said before: Every baby and mom is different. One size does not fit all when it comes to a preferred cloth diaper brand.

Look for quality. There are tons of diapers on the market, so you'll have to decide if you want to work with a known brand name with established manufacturing processes or a small cottage or home-based business that likely hand sews each diaper. You'll also want to decide between fasteners such as snaps (more durable and long-lasting but takes extra time to fasten) or Velcro-style hooks and loops (wears faster but provides for quicker diaper changes).

Warranties. Always be sure to check out a manufacturer's warranty and find one you can live with. I know that a manufacturer who stands behind its product for at least a year offers some peace of mind and assurance to the newbie cloth diaperer.

☑ How Many Cloth Diapers Do You Need?

Figuring out how many diapers you'll need depends on a few things:

- ☑ Your baby's age
- ☑ How often you want to do laundry
- ☑ Your preference toward changing your baby's diaper

As a mother who cloth diapers, I recommend that you keep about 18 to 24 diapers on hand if you plan on washing every other day, although some moms get by with about 12 and others prefer to have closer to 24 and even 36. You can anticipate washing your diapers every 2 to 3 days, so you'll want to have a large enough stash to make this happen.

Babies from birth to 3 months will go through more diapers on a daily basis—10 to 14—and you may feel as if you're constantly doing laundry if you don't have a stash to last you about 2 days. But I assure you that as baby gets more active, he or she won't require as many diaper changes and you won't need as large of a stash.

I recommend that you keep about 18 to 24 diapers on hand if you plan on washing every other day.

Buying a few extra diapers means you can do larger loads of laundry less frequently. This will save you time, money, and energy, which is good for you, the planet, and your wallet.

Here are some general guidelines:

☑ Newborn to 4 months: 20 to 24 diapers

☑ Infant (4 to 10 months): 16 to 20 diapers

☑ Toddler (10 months to potty training): 12 to 16 diapers

VELCRO-STYLE OR SNAPS?
THE DEBATE STICKS AROUND

The heated debate in Cloth Diaperville is whether it's better to use cloth diapers that have Velcro-style or snap fasteners. Avoid making a snap decision when it comes to Velcro-style or snaps.

The simple truth is that it's a matter of preference. Each fastener has its unique set of pros and cons.

Fluffy Stuff!

Don't "size up" when purchasing cloth diapers. When purchasing clothing for baby, many people size up to extend the length of the wearing time. You don't want to size up with diapers because this can cause leaking and a poor fit.

Velcro-style Pros

- May lead to quicker diaper changes since you just have to pull the Velcro-style tabs on baby (similar to disposable diapers). Quicker than snaps.

- More adjustability to give the most custom fit possible. You are not limited by where the fasteners fall on the diaper.

- Often said to be easier to use. People not used to cloth diapering (your daycare provider or dad) may find it easier to use Velcro-style since they're the most like disposables.

Velcro-style Cons

- May not last as long because even normal wear and tear makes the diapers' Velcro-style fasteners wear out in an average of twelve to fourteen months.

- You must remember to use the laundry tabs (the fastener tabs must be folded down to cover the hook tabs before washing) so they don't snag other diapers in the wash (remember, you don't wash cloth diapers with other clothing).

- Velcro-style fasteners can curl when washed and aren't as smooth under baby's clothing as snaps.

- More difficult to re-sell since the Velcro-style fasteners wear out more easily.

- A toddler can easily pull off the Velcro-style tabs if he or she becomes curious about the colorful cloth diaper.

Snap Pros

- Last a long time because the snaps rarely wear out.

- Can be easier to re-sell since they don't look "used".

- Snaps are always smooth under baby's clothing with no curls or snags to contend with.

- Snaps allow for three to four levels of adjustability.

- No need to worry about laundry tabs. Just toss diapers in the wash when soiled. Snaps won't snag the other diapers.

- Very durable and strong. Most babies can't undo them on their own should they become curious about their super cool cloth diaper.

Snap Cons

- Snap fasteners offer a varying fit, which can be challenging if your baby is between snap sizes.

- Can take a bit longer to change (a sometimes squirmy) baby because you have to snap three to five snaps in a single diaper change.

- Can deter a newbie diapering spouse or partner from using cloth diapers because they require a little more patience, especially up front.

🌼 Fluffy Stuff!

The Velcro-style fasteners are shot on some of my diapers. Can I fix those?

Many manufacturers offer Velcro-style replacement kits either free of charge or for a nominal fee. But first check to see if your cloth diaper manufacturer offers a warranty period, so if your closures fail during a certain time period, they will replace or repair your diapers. Find out on the packaging or at the manufacturer's website.

You can also have your diapers with Velcro-style closures converted to snap closures. A site that specializes in this service is www.MakeitSnappy.ca.

"I feel savvy, trendy, and smart, and my son looks totally fashionable!"

—A.F., Omaha, Nebraska

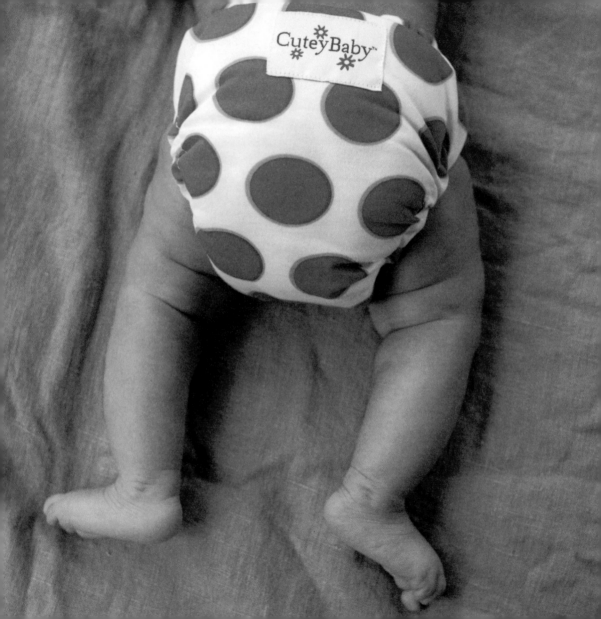

CHAPTER 4

FROM NEWBORN TO TODDLER:

DIAPERING FOR THE AGES AND STAGES

Cloth diapering a tiny newborn baby is much different than diapering a squirmy busy-body tot. Here are some tips for cloth diapering a baby at any age.

What Moms Say... about "getting started"

"I'm certain had I started cloth diapering right after my son was born, I would have given up. We started after he was already settled and my hormones were back to normal!" says Lisa M. ●

NEWBORNS TO THREE MONTHS

Cloth diapering a newborn can be challenging for many reasons. For one, a newborn's bowel movements take a few days to regulate. Baby's first few poops will be what is called meconium, a tar-like first poop. You probably don't want meconium on a cloth diaper because it will stick and stain it, and it may be difficult to wash off.

I recommend that you consider using disposable liners during the first few days of baby's life. This way the diapers are easier to clean and don't get ruined at first use.

Second, a newborn is so little and may not fit in a bulkier cloth diaper right away—even one-sized diapers don't properly fit a baby until the baby is about 7.5 or 8 pounds. Don't be discouraged if your little one doesn't fit into cloth diapers right away. He or she will grow fast and your diaper will fit in a few weeks, before you know it!

If you have a very small baby or preemie, consider getting diapers that come in extra small (XS). It's likely the XS will fit for several weeks until baby grows.

Fluffy Stuff!

Beware that baby's umbilical cord can take up to two weeks to fall off. Cloth diapers may be bulky on the baby and irritate the baby's belly button. Use your judgment whether to wait to use cloth diapers until baby's umbilical cord has come free. Check out Rump•a•rooz Lil Joey diapers. They have an umbilical cord front snap down! You can also fold over other brands so they don't irritate the belly button too.

Third, keep in mind that newborns go through many more diapers than older babies and toddlers. Expect to be changing ten to fourteen diapers daily (whether baby is in cloth or disposable diapers)—and doing more laundry during these first few months. It gets easier, trust me!

Next, let's talk about baby's poop after your newborn has finished the meconium stage. It's not solid, rather it's a yellowish liquidy mess. Don't worry, you can wash these diapers in your machine with no problems. Hey, no need to plop the poop into the toilet just yet! Honestly, these newborn bowel movements wash out very easily.

And finally, don't commit to one brand or type too soon. Many parents are eager to buy cloth diapers before their baby arrives, but try out a few brands for yourself (remember what works for one baby doesn't work for another) and see what you like. Pockets or all-in-ones (AIOs) are typically the easiest to get started with, but you may find that you like fitteds too and want to diversify your stash.

FOUR MONTHS TO ONE YEAR

By the fourth month, your baby has gained some weight and the cloth diapers are probably fitting just fine on the small to medium settings. It's likely you've also gained some confidence and have your routine down pat. Good for you!

Also by this time, some moms go back to work, which presents its own set of challenges. See chapter 5 to learn some strategies for getting your daycare provider on board with your cloth diapering routine.

ONE YEAR AND UP

If you're cloth diapering an older baby, you likely have your routine down to a science and can change a cloth diaper in just a few seconds. You may also find that you don't need to change your baby as frequently as they get older.

At this time you'll also notice that baby's poop is changing as you add more solids and variety to baby's diet. You'll want to make sure you're plopping and flushing solid poop (even the mushy stuff) down the toilet—and it's a good idea to invest in a diaper sprayer attachment for those extra messy poopy disasters. Another option is a biodegradable, flushable liner. These essentially are paper liners that act as "poop catchers." Bummis flushable liners are super soft. Even disposable diaper manufacturers recommend you flush poops down the toilet before tossing in the trash, but nobody does that.

Fluffy Stuff!

Getting the right size diaper is very important because you don't want a bulky mess hidden under your baby's clothes, and you don't want them to be too tight so that they leak all the time. Every manufacturer has specific instructions related to sizing that involve measuring your baby's waist, rise, and legs.

Follow these instructions carefully to get the best fit.

Waist: Measure baby naked using the belly button as your level.

Rise: Measure from your baby's belly button, between their legs, and back up to the same place on their backside.

Legs: Measure around the fullest part of the thigh.

As a cloth diapering mom, you may face a variety of challenges and scenarios not faced by your disposable diaper counterparts as you think about going back to work and turning over your fluffy-bottomed baby to daycare providers. It may be helpful to know that you're not alone. Many moms before you went through similar situations.

I'd like to share some special scenarios with you in the next few chapters to help guide you through these processes with ease.

CHAPTER 5

THE BACK-TO-WORK AND DAYCARE DIAPERING DILEMMA

Parents often face obstacles to cloth diapering when they go back to work. Daycare settings prefer the convenience of disposable diapers and have several misconceptions about cloth diapering.

A Real Diaper Association study found that women were able to get past daycare naysayers with a little education and passion on the topic. Talk to your daycare provider openly and honestly about why you use reusable diapers and how you'd like to continue doing so when your baby is in their care.

Many parents encounter much resistance when they try to push cloth diapers into their daycare centers, but we have learned that many daycares simply don't know about modern cloth diaper options.

Here are some strategies to get past "no" when your daycare provider poo poos the idea:

- **Seeing is believing.** Bring in your AIO or pocket diaper and show the provider just how easy they are to use and store after each diaper change.

- **Let's try it.** Offer to do a trial period with the center to see how it works and if they can make it work long-term. A temporary commitment is better than a permanent "no way," so most will be open to trying first.

- **Legal opinions.** If your daycare provider says it's against the law for daycares to use cloth diapers, remind the provider that you understand their concern and you did some research ahead of time. You will need to check your state's laws on cloth diapers (check the National Resource Center for Health and Safety in Child Care and Early Education at http://nrckids.org).

Here's a sampling of what I found for each state. Only one of the four states I researched more in depth disallows cloth diapers unless there is a medical reason for it:

- **California:** 101428 INFANT CARE PERSONAL SERVICES "Soiled or wet clothing or cloth diapers provided by the infant's authorized representative shall be placed in an airtight container and returned to the authorized representative at the end of each day. The airtight container shall prevent the escape of fluids and odors and be portable enough to give to the authorized representative."

- **Colorado:** 8-404 "Soiled cloth diapers shall be immediately placed in a waterproof bag after being removed from the child and shall be stored in a covered diaper pail for return to the parents, guardians or diaper service or until laundered. Soiled cloth diapers or clothing shall not be rinsed."

- **Maine:** 22.5.6. "Child Care Facilities using cloth diapers must comply with diapering guidelines available from the Department of Health and Human Services, Division of Licensing and Regulatory Services. Cloth diapers may be used only when the child has a medical reason that does not permit the use of disposable diapers (such as allergic reactions). The child's health care provider must document the medical reason. The documentation must be placed in the Child Care Facility's file." 22.5.7. "All containers of soiled cloth or disposable diapers must be removed daily from the childcare areas."

- **Missouri:** 19 CSR 30-62.182 "Wet or soiled diapers shall be placed in an airtight disposal container located in the diaper change area. If cloth diapers are provided by the parent(s), individual airtight plastic bags shall be used to store each soiled diaper for return each day to the parent(s)."

If you are using cloth diapers for a medical reason and you have a valid doctor's note saying as much, your daycare provider will need to work with you to cloth diaper your baby. If you feel your baby's sensitive skin requires round-the-clock cloth diaper love, then let your doctor know and most will be willing to write that doctor's note for you within reason.

✓ Cloth Diaper–Friendly Daycare Directory

The Real Diaper Association in partnership with the Real Diaper Industry Association (RDIA) has a Cloth Diaper Friendly Daycare Directory, which lists daycares across the United States and Canada that support cloth diapering families. This list, found online at www.RealDiaperAssociation.org, is updated by parents who are sharing their experiences with others. The list grows each day.

What Moms Say... about "cloth diapering and daycare"

"The first few months of cloth diapering went well so we were sold on them by the time I went back to work. The trick was figuring out how to 'sell' daycare on using the cloth diapers I provided.

"I thought long and hard about how I would talk to my daycare about it and decided to treat it as something easy for them to do and not a potential problem. So I did not ask if we could cloth diaper because I figured that would set the conversation on a path

I wanted to avoid. Instead, when visiting them the week before we started with them, I said very nonchalantly, 'Oh, and by the way we cloth diaper, so what do we need to do to make that work here?'

"They were a bit surprised (we were the first family to approach them about cloth diapering), but took it in stride. They asked what cloth diapering entailed and how I thought it would go best.

"Their main concern was the appropriate storage/disposal of human waste given state laws regulating daycares. They wanted a sanitary way to package each used diaper. I had thought about this and presented this solution: We all agreed that bringing in diapers each day and providing small wet bags for each diaper and a larger wet bag to store all of them would work best. I bought some tiny wet bags and a medium-sized wet bag and we were in business.

"I spent some time teaching my daughter's daycare teachers how to use them, but that was a breeze. Although they were a little hesitant at first, after a few weeks they were in a groove and I even had one of the teachers asking me for an in-depth lesson in cloth because she was considering using them for her baby," says Berkeley Y. of North Carolina. [More on wet bags in chapter 10.] ●

"Several years ago a mom approached me about cloth diapering her son while he was in my care. I told her that I'd be happy to give it a try if she gave me instructions on how to do it. I must admit, I was intrigued by cloth diapers and had heard about them when my older daughter was near potty training. I knew I wanted to try them for my second baby so I figured trying it out on a baby in my daycare would be a great way to get some hands-on experience and to see if I'd like doing it after all.

"This particular mom wanted to use the most cost-effective diapers around, so she used prefolds with Thirsties covers. When I first started using cloth diapers on the baby in my daycare, I didn't find it as gross and messy as I thought it would be. I was simply throwing the dirty diapers in the mom's wet bag and sending them home for her to take care of. I did find, however, that my assistants weren't as open to the idea; I ended up changing most of this baby's diapers. That said, I was proud of myself for sticking with it and the whole process showed me how easy it truly was. Overall, it gave me the confidence to try it with my next baby!

"I think many moms are scared to ask their daycare provider to use cloth diapers. But if you ask you may be surprised that many are willing to give it a try," says Kathryn P., a San Marcos, California, mom of two and in-home daycare provider. ●

"I don't know if I would say I had to convince my daycare provider to use cloth diapers … in all honesty, all I had to do was ask her if it's something she'd be willing to do. She right away said, 'Sure, I've done it for other moms.' I thought that was great!

"The night before I sent cloth diapers to daycare for the first time, I called my daycare provider to see what she required of me (like how many diapers she wanted, wet bags and so on). During our conversation I learned that the last time she dealt with cloth diapers was fifteen years ago! Of course fifteen years ago she was working with prefolds and covers. Instead of a wet bag, the moms sent a five-gallon bucket with lid. I knew right away my daycare provider was in for a nice surprise.

"The next day rolled around and I decided we'd jump right in, full force, instead of my initial plan of easing her into it. Before daycare I put my son in a cloth diaper, I packed three additional cloth diapers, a wet bag and two spare outfits and we were out the door!

"When we got to daycare I showed my provider one of the cloth diapers; she was obviously impressed with the quality of the diaper as well as how far cloth has come in general. I explained the importance of the Velcro placement and what to do if he broke out in diaper rash. I then left and went to work.

"Midday I sent her a text asking her if she had any problems with them and of course she texted back, 'No, not at all!' To tell you the truth, I wasn't surprised. Cloth diapers are easy and she was open-minded from the start. Two weeks have gone by and we're still successfully cloth diapering with no problems," says Barbara W., a Newark, Delaware, mom. ●

"Cloth diapering at our daycare makes me feel like everyone in my daughter's life is on the same page. Thanks to the other moms for joining the movement too!"

—H.M.T., Fayetteville, North Carolina

TRAVELING WITH CLOTH DIAPERS

Yes, you can travel with cloth diapers!

If you have access to a washing machine

First you need to determine whether you will have access to a washing machine. If you do, here are a few tips:

- If you are staying with a relative or friend, I recommend shipping a box of kids' clothes and diapers ahead of time. The shipping cost will actually be cheaper than having to pay for an additional bag you might have to check with an airline. The key is to pack a diaper system that will dry quickly. Hybrid systems like Flip, GroVia, or gDiapers have a simple cover and either a cloth or an eco-friendly disposable option.

- Pack enough diapers for two days of diapering. First, determine how many times you change baby a day. If you change six times, then you want to have at least twelve diapers if you wash every other day. If you choose the hybrid diaper system, you can pack twelve cloth inserts and four covers.

- Pack samples of cloth diaper–friendly detergent with your shipping box. This way you don't have to worry (or ask) if your host has detergent that is safe for cloth diapers.

If you don't have access to a washing machine

If you don't have access to a washing machine, this is a good plan:

- Pack a hybrid diaper system. Usually four covers is enough.

- If you use the eco-friendly disposable inserts, be sure to figure out how many days you will be gone and multiply that by the approximate number of changes per day.

- If you want to go completely with cloth diapers, pack enough cloth diaper inserts so you only have to hand wash the inserts every third day. Take the number of diaper changes per day and multiply that by three and that will give the amount you need. To make hand washing easier, pack some biodegradable, flushable liners. Put a liner in every diaper and this will get most of the bowel movements. Then you are essentially hand washing inserts that only have pee.

- Another option is to use flat-style diapers inside your covers. These wash super easy and dry very quickly.

- Pack samples of cloth diaper–friendly detergent. These hardly take up any space and are usually safe for TSA guidelines. (Be sure to check ahead of time for TSA restrictions/requirements.)

If you decide not to use cloth diapers while traveling, don't feel guilty. You choose what is best for you and your baby.

USING CLOTH DIAPERS IN THE HOSPITAL

Your initial reaction might be, "You have got to be kidding me—using cloth diapers in hospitals?"

Now that you know more about modern cloth diapers, you can use cloth diapers right from birth. Many hospitals are now willing to let parents bring in cloth diapers to use as long as you change your baby.

Be sure to check with your hospital to see if cloth diapers are allowed. If they aren't, you can advocate for yourself by doing the following:

- Bring in samples of cloth diapers. I suggest bringing in an all-in-one style (AIO) or pocket-style diaper. The best place to do this is to bring the cloth diapers to one of your childbirth education classes.

- Let them know that you are willing (or your spouse or partner is willing) to change all the diapers.

- Ask a local cloth diaper retailer to see if they would be able to contact the hospital on your behalf. This might be an opportunity for a cloth diaper retailer to suggest offering a cloth diapering class as part of (or separate from) the hospital's childbirth education classes.

- Recruit advocates. Contact the Real Diaper Association (www.RealDiaperAssociation.org) for helpful tips. They also have advocacy pamphlets available on their site that you can print from your home computer. Visit the advocacy group called Cloth Diapers in Hospitals (www.ClothDiapersinHospitals.blogspot.com) and on Facebook (www.facebook.com/ClothinHospitals) for support on how you can advocate for the use of cloth diapers in hospitals.

CHAPTER 6

AND BABY MAKES TWO (OR MORE):
CLOTH DIAPERING MULTIPLES AND OTHER SPECIAL LITTLE ONES

Cloth diapering twins or triplets (or more) at a time can be an experience, in and of itself, according to most moms of multiples I know. However, some say that cloth diapering twins might actually be easier on mom, kinder to Mother Earth, and easier on the wallet. After all, you get nearly double the cost savings!

What Moms Say... about "twins"

"I finally decided to switch to cloth diapers for a few reasons. One, my sons kept leaking out of disposables. Every single disposable I put on them leaked overnight. He was not getting enough rest, and neither was I. Something had to give.

"The second reason was I was tired of wasting money. I also realized that I was throwing out three thirteen-gallon-sized garbage bags almost full of disposables every week. It was disgusting!" says Melina S., Oklahoma City mom of twins. She switched to cloth diapers when the twins were ten months old. Melina estimates that she spent about $80 on disposable diapers per month and was buying them by the bulk at her discount wholesale club. ●

HOW MANY DIAPERS
SHOULD A MOM OF TWINS BUY?

Diapering twins means you'll go through double the amount of diapers in one day, although you'll wash all the diapers together, possibly doing the same amount of "diaper" laundry as a mother of just one baby.

One of the moms of twin boys recommends that a mom of twins have at least twelve diapers per child so you only have to do laundry every other day. She admits that she started with twelve diapers total and was doing laundry daily, which she says is "exhausting." Ideally, she says, forty cloth diapers is the "perfect" amount for mothers of twins so you don't have to wash them daily.

Fluffy Stuff!

If you and your friend(s) are having babies around the same time and want to use cloth diapers, consider placing your order for diapers together. Many online retailers offer bulk discounts and together you can save more than you would alone.

WHAT BRANDS ARE BEST FOR MULTIPLES?

I rely on an expert mom of twins who says that one-size diapers work well for twins because they can easily be sized up and down for each baby (in case one baby is bigger than the other). She says she has a few sized diapers because her son is a "big boy."

If you have one boy and one girl, choose gender-neutral diaper colors, except for the times you want to dress your boy in boy colors and your girl a little more girly.

"But that doesn't mean that my son doesn't sometimes wear purple or a pale pink on laundry day when I'm at the bottom of the pile!" says one mom of twins.

"Cloth diapering twins is the only way to go!
No trips to the store in the middle of the night,
no icky rashes, and lots of cute bums around!"

—E.P., St. Joseph, Michigan

What Moms Say... **about "going green"**

"Over the past few years, I've been getting more into the whole green lifestyle. My husband and I had slowly been making changes to our lives. When we found out we were pregnant, I started researching cloth diapers. Not only did I hate the thought of sending off all those disposable diapers to live forever in a landfill, I knew they were expensive. After finding out we were having twins, I was even more interested in cloth diapers.

"After doing a lot of online research, I decided we would start out with prefolds and covers. If we felt it was doable, we would then agree to try some one-size diapers. From what I'd read, if we used a one-size cloth diaper from birth to potty-training, that would be the life of the diaper," says Summer K., mom of twins who cloth diapered her twin boy and girl starting at three weeks. ●

SPECIAL NEEDS BABIES ARE FINE WITH CLOTH

Some babies with special needs require special attention. I'll let Janet C., a mom from Troy, Mich., tell you about her son, Alexander. He was born early at twenty-seven weeks when Janet developed pre-eclampsia and needed an emergency C-section.

Alexander needed a lot of help breathing, which eventually led to a tracheotomy and bringing him home with a ventilator. Here's her story:

"I decided to use cloth diapers long before Alexander was born. We'd always planned to use cloth. Both my husband and I were cloth diapered as babies. We live in an area with curbside recycling, and our recycle bins are usually fuller than our trash cans. I couldn't stand the thought of another trash can every week just for diapers. Plus, I cringed when I thought about all the money we'd be spending on them.

"My husband and I make a decent living, but we both grew up without a lot of money so we're picky about what we spend our money on, and disposable diapers were not something either of us wanted to waste our hard-earned money on week after week.

"I also knew cloth diapers would be good for my son's overall health. Babies in disposables don't get changed as often because they don't *feel* wet. This leaves urine to linger on their skin longer than it should be there.

"Because Alexander was born premature, he was in the NICU for almost ten months. At first, we didn't think he'd be there that long, and diapers were the last thing on our mind, but as time went on, we started asking about changing to cloth.

"When Alexander was a few months old, he developed a horrible diaper rash. He had bright cherry red skin across his entire bottom and onto his tiny thighs. We tried many things to get the rash under control and we knew cloth diapers would help. We thought this would be our shot at making it happen, but the nurses and doctors were not biting, even though one of the nurse practitioners and several of our primary nurses agreed with us.

"In our case, the doctors and nurses said no to cloth diapers because Alexander was on diuretics. They were closely monitoring his intake of fluids and how much he was peeing each day. They feared that cloth diapers would be difficult to manage with that system because they calculated his urine output by the weight of his diaper. Although we were unable to convince them to use cloth diapers, we were able to get the doctor to switch his formula, which resolved his rash problem in a few days.

"When we took Alexander home, we finally had control over his diapering situation. We use cloth exclusively now, other than during hospital stays. We have rotating nurses come to our house and care for him every day, and they are all open to using cloth. Eventually, when Alexander no longer has a trach tube, we won't have nursing help, and we'll be adamant about finding a daycare that takes cloth. I think we are well positioned to make that work given the obstacles we've already had to overcome.

"Alexander is doing well at home, but every time he has to go back in the hospital, I wondered why I hated the smell of hospital stench. I recently realized at our last hospital visit that the 'stench' is the smell of disposable diapers … the odor is strong enough to remind me why I'm never going back to disposables."

"Cloth diapering makes me feel like a Super Mom!
A super-green-awesome-loving mom!"

—J.A. Phoenix, Arizona

CHAPTER 7

CONQUERING LEAKS, RASHES, AND THE NIGHTTIME WET MESS

Although cloth diapers absorb very well, you cannot leave baby in a diaper for four to five hours during the day and expect the diaper not to leak. It is important to change your baby frequently.

CLOTH DIAPERS LEAK, DON'T THEY?

Cloth diapers aren't fool-proof and have issues that will frustrate a mom from time to time, just like anything else. Cloth diapers leak for three main reasons. So let's wade through this soggy mess and put your mind at rest.

Absorbency

First, it's important to change your baby frequently. Although cloth diapers absorb very well, you cannot leave baby in a diaper for four to five hours during the day and expect the diaper not to leak. It's simple science: if a diaper becomes saturated, it will inevitably leak.

To prevent leaks caused by absorbency issues, be sure to change your baby every two to three hours (whether in cloth or disposables) or as needed (usually more often for younger babies and less often for older babies).

If your baby is a super soaker, you may consider adding additional absorbency to prevent leaks. Bamboo, hemp inserts, or doublers will provide you with the best absorption possible. Some suggestions include Swaddlebees Bamboo Doublers, Knickernappies Loopy-Do Prewashed Hemp Inserts, or Thirsties Hemp Inserts.

See the Nighttime Wet Mess section later in this chapter for troubleshooting nighttime leaks.

Size

Diapers that don't properly fit your baby may also be the culprit in why your baby's diapers leak. Diapers that are too small may not have enough room to properly absorb your baby's urine output, and a diaper that is too big will not hug your baby's curves enough to prevent leaking from the leg casings.

One-size diapers can be easily adjusted to create more or less room. But if your baby is really big (let's say, larger than thirty-five pounds), you may need to consider large or extra-large-sized diapers.

On the other end of the spectrum, it's important to note that newborns don't typically fit a one-size diaper very well from day one. You can try using an extra-small-sized diaper in the early weeks until baby has had time to grow into the one-size diapers. These diapers are also perfect for preemies.

Residue Buildup

Leaks can also be caused by residue buildup. Many commercial detergents billed as "free and clear" can cause detergent/soap buildup on your diapers and may cause your diapers to repel moisture—the opposite of their intended use. The only place for repelled moisture to go is out of the diapers because it won't get properly absorbed by the fabrics.

Another way to create residue buildup on diapers is by using fabric softeners (a no-no in cloth diapering) or an oily/petroleum-based diaper cream. Never use either! If your baby has a rash and requires a cream treatment, be sure to use a liner over your cloth diaper to prevent it from getting contaminated with oily residue.

Remember, approved cloth diaper–friendly detergents will reduce your chances of detergent residue buildup because they are free from enzymes, dyes, fragrances, and fabric softeners. See washing instructions discussed in depth in chapter 9.

BREAK OUT THIS RASH OF INFORMATION

Jana G. from Bartlett, Tenn., says that she never considered cloth diapers until her son's painful and frightening reaction to disposable diapers caused her to take a closer look. Here's what she told me:

"When my son was six months old, he began developing a raised bumpy rash in his diaper area and on his inner thighs. Over the course of a few weeks the rash on his thighs got larger and more inflamed until his thighs were on the verge of bleeding. You could tell that his disposable diapers really bothered him and his thighs and bottom looked inflamed and very painful. As a new mother, it was upsetting to see my baby in so much pain and not know how to help him. I felt helpless.

"His doctor told me he had dermatitis and eczema. She said my son had a severe allergy to either one of the materials or the chemicals used in the production of disposables. We also learned that dermatitis itches very badly, although our son was too young to tell us that it bothered him as much as it probably did.

"Our doctor prescribed hydrocortisone cream to treat the inflammation. Also, to our surprise, she recommended that we switch to cloth diapers at least until the rash cleared up.

"I quickly began researching a variety of cloth diapers to learn about my options. I was quite overwhelmed and very surprised at the number of options, brands, and cloth diapering stores available. After much research, I settled on the FuzziBunz Perfect Sized diapers exclusively, but have since expanded our collection to use GroBaby and bumGenius one-size too. (I found that I love buying new cloth diapers and am hooked!)

"Between the hydrocortisone and the switch to cloth diapers, my son's skin showed immediate improvement and cleared up completely within a couple of weeks. Seeing my son no longer in pain and almost in a state of relief was enough to keep me cloth diapering for good.

"Today, almost two years later, we have two kids in cloth. My son is now twenty-three months and he will wear cloth until he potty trains. My ten-week-old daughter has been in cloth since she was three weeks old, and I have no plans to put her in disposables and risk her getting dermatitis. Plus, I simply love cloth diapering. There's no going back!"

CONQUER THE NIGHTTIME WET MESS

Finding the right overnight cloth diaper can be a challenge for some moms, but persistence pays off and most mamas I talked with say they certainly have their preferred diaper for overnight success.

To prevent your baby from waking up in a wet mess, consider these nighttime cloth diapering tips I've gleaned along the way:

Go pockets. Because pockets enable you to customize the absorbency, hands down this type of diaper is the overwhelming nighttime choice for mothers.

Try various brands. What works for one baby often doesn't work for another. Mothers have sworn by bumGenius, FuzziBunz, or Happy Heinys for overnight success, but the list of popular brands preferred for nighttime use goes on and on. If one brand fails you at night, try another. The right one for your little baby may only be a "try" away!

Double up on inserts. For those pocket diaper fans out there, moms say that while the micro-terry insert is just fine for daytime absorption, overnight protection requires two inserts.

Try hemp. Many moms find hemp to be even more absorbent than micro-terry, plus hemp has antibacterial and odor-fighting properties, making it especially appealing for nighttime use.

Use a combo of hemp and micro-terry. Some moms say that while hemp is super absorbent, it doesn't absorb as fast. So a combination of one hemp and one micro-terry insert inside the pocket of the diaper meets both tasks head on! If you are using a hemp and micro-terry insert inside a pocket diaper, always put the micro-terry insert on top (closer to baby) and the hemp insert on the bottom. Micro-terry wicks moisture quickly and you will want this to be the first insert that baby's urine hits.

"I feel proud, because I know I am doing the most natural and safe thing for my son."

—A.K., Rockford, Illinois

CHAPTER 8

DADDIES AND DIAPERS

If dad needs convincing (because he's going to be doing his fair share of changing diapers too), start your conversation with this: "Honey, how would you like to save $2,500?"

Moms are usually the first to be on board with cloth diapers. Once Mom is convinced, then it usually takes a bit to convince dads that modern cloth diapering can save the family money, is eco-friendly, and better for the baby.

If Dad needs convincing (because he's going to be doing his fair share of changing diapers too), start your conversation with this: "Honey, how would you like to save $2,500?"

As his head swims with the idea that he really might be able to get that big-screen TV after all the unanticipated costs of having a baby are added up, he could be brought on board rather quickly. Yet some guys take more convincing. And some never ever want to change diapers no matter what.

Don't force the issue. But why don't you leave this book near his favorite spot (maybe in the bathroom or by the TV remote) and put a bookmark right here on this chapter. Let him read what other men say about this diapering issue.

What Moms Say... about "dads and diapering"

"I was afraid my husband wouldn't be too crazy about cloth diapering—and rightfully so! Not only were we having twins, but also we were going to be first-time parents. I decided that if anything might sway him to being supportive of cloth diapers it would be to show him how much we would save. I remember vividly the day I first brought up the subject. I was about six months pregnant. I had found a website that did the math for me, and I had printed out some information along with calculations about how much we'd save—times two!

"He was very much against it and wasn't interested in hearing anything more about it. We still had plenty of time before the babies were due, so I just continued to read about cloth diapers and research them online. A little closer to their due date, I broached the subject again. I talked about how we could get a starter kit of prefolds and covers and even if we only used them for a few weeks, we wouldn't be out any money. I also suggested we wait a few weeks after the babies were born to start.

"When the babies were three weeks old, I ordered two starter kits of prefolds, Snappis, and covers. It's funny, after I'd done all this research about which diapers to start with, I was paralyzed with fear about washing them. I finally found a detergent I could use to wash them, I prepped them, and shortly thereafter we started our journey.

"At first, we didn't have enough cloth diapers on hand to do it full-time. But after a couple weeks of using what we had, we decided we were ready to do it full-time and ordered enough prefolds for a full day. I was really surprised by how easy it was and how into the whole process my husband got. Before I knew it, he was telling other people about how easy it was.

"A month or so later, we did a trial of cloth diapers and I really liked the one-size pockets, mainly these brands: Blueberry, bumGenius, FuzziBunz, and Happy Heinys.

"Our twin babies wear different size diapers so we have two baskets on our changing table and we just keep them separated. My daughter wears mainly FuzziBunz diapers and my son wears bumGenius diapers. I find it fascinating that different brand cloth diapers just fit them so differently and one brand works better for one of my babies over the other," says Summer K. ●

What Dads Say... about "being a cloth diapering dude"

Richard is a stay-at-home dad who lives in Powell River on the Sunshine Coast of British Columbia, Canada. And, yes, he cloth diapers and likes it too! With five children in the house—two of them in diapers—his household is one busy place to be. Here's what this stay-at-home dad thinks of cloth diapers and why he considers himself a fan:

"Since August 2008 I have been a full-time stay-at-home-dad. My wife, Char, had already been home with her first three children (from a previous marriage) and was more than happy to let me stay home to raise our kids while she could develop her career. I had always dreamed of the idea of being the one to stay home with my children. We both consider ourselves lucky to be where we want to be.

"Our first experience with cloth diapers was with our daughter. We tried a hybrid reusable diaper, which involved a washable outer pant and a flushable/disposable insert. We found the whole process cumbersome and costly, and eventually abandoned the idea of using cloth diapers altogether. Convenience is important to me as I keep up with five children and all the chores that come with it. I don't want to be wasting time messing around with complicated and time-consuming diapers.

"Over a year later, while on a trip to visit family, we were introduced to the concept of cloth diapering again through my cousin. She has a collection of bumGenius one-size cloth diapers. Char was immediately interested in the concept as they were very different from the diapers we originally tried and looked nothing like the traditional old cloth diapers our parents were raised in. I was still skeptical of the whole process.

"We stayed with my cousin long enough to give her cloth diapers a try. We were very impressed with the results. It didn't take long to realize that the cost of the cloth diapers would be offset with the savings from no longer buying disposables. And these types of cloth diapers were environmentally responsible, which I liked.

"My wife immediately set out to find out what was available in cloth diapers beyond the ones we tried at my cousin's house. She found a local woman in Edmonton who provided a sampling of a variety of cloth diaper options that we could try for a small fee. After we tried several types and brands, we decided that we liked all-in-ones and the Bummis starter package was the best choice for us. We liked that we were able to sample many before committing to one. We realized we had committed to the hybrid concept too quickly and it soured us on cloth diapering in general. We didn't take the time to learn about other cloth diapers and options.

"Now I freely admit that I'm a cloth diapering dude! I enjoy that I'm not creating a lot of waste and that we're not putting chemicals up against our baby's skin. I also have to admit that I really enjoy the diaper sprayer we've hooked up on our toilet to rinse off soiled diapers. What man can resist hosing down anything with a stream of high-pressure water!

"I also really like saving money. If you sit down to do the math, it won't take a dad long to realize that cloth diapering is the best way to go. All in all, cloth diapering is time and money well spent." ●

What Moms Say... about "guys doing diapers"

Alycia C. of Springfield, Mass., says she was surprised how her boyfriend, Tom, supported—and even embraced—cloth diapers.

She says her boyfriend is a "sort-of stay-at-home-dad" because during the summer months he's a landscaper and in the winter he's a part-time police officer a few nights per week. He's home most days between those jobs.

Alycia says it was her idea to try cloth and that Tom didn't really care at first.

"He just rolled his eyes and thought it was another one of my crazy ideas. But once he saw that I was serious and was sticking to it, he got much more comfortable with the idea," she says.

Tom didn't do much diaper changing in the beginning since Alycia was home most of the time. Over time, she says Tom discovered that AIOs were his diaper of choice and that unlike most other cloth diapering dads she's known, her boyfriend had a strong preference for snaps over Velcro because they look new and clean—and are less work than Velcro because you don't have to worry about the laundry tabs.

She says, "One day, out of the blue, my boyfriend, who is 100 percent Italian, asked me if we could have a custom Italian cloth diaper made. That's when I knew he was officially hooked!"

She also says that she loves that Tom sometimes brags about his cloth diapering knowledge.

"We were at our friend's house one night when Tommy needed to be changed. I changed him and our friend said, 'Oh here, let me throw that out for you.' Of course he looked surprised when I told him Tommy's diapers were cloth. Afterward, Tom told our friend about how great cloth diapers are, how we had custom Italian diapers made, how we save money, etc. He certainly said enough to make him sound like a true cloth diapering daddy!" ●

What Dads Say... **about a diapering epiphany (*e-poo-phany*)**

As a single dad, I didn't really have anyone guiding me in my decision to cloth diaper. It was more of an epiphany actually. I was at the park with my six-month-old son taking in the summer breeze and breathing the sweet smelling flowers and trees. As we turned around the bend where we always stop to rest, a swirling stench filled the air from the nearby trash can, stealing away the fresh air like the Grinch wrapping up the Christmas tree and shoving it up the chimney.

At that moment, I realized that it might actually be my own son's diaper from two days before. There it was, smelling up the world, preserved among the other trash in a disposable diaper time capsule so well built that it would outlive my son and me, and probably a few more generations.

The next instant, I heard the voices of three moms I had met a month earlier spinning around in my head about cloth diapering. At the time, I dismissed cloth diapering as an unrealistic choice. Didn't only hippies and earth mothers use those? But those moms kept saying that the new diapers were different. *But different than what?* I struggle enough trying to get my squirmy little guy into those onesies. And the sleepers! How many snaps do you think I can handle?

I have to admit, I did check out their babies, and they were all wearing what appeared to be colorful puffy underwear. I remember thinking, "Those rear ends would give JLo a run for her money!"

That day, I went to a store looking for cloth diapers. I found one that looked like a dish towel, and one that was a huge piece of white fabric. I ended up buying a package of each and taking them home. There were no instructions, and they didn't look anywhere near like the ones the moms at the park had on their kids. *It must be a secret that only moms know. Where do they get those adorable cloth diapers and how do they get them to stay on?*

That first day, I tried tucking, tying, and bundling, but those didn't work. Hint: Painter's tape does work in a pinch, but is not recommended!

So that night, I sat down and Googled "cloth diapers." Aha! What I had purchased were "prefolds." I needed pins and covers to make these diapers work. Then I knew what was important to make this journey successful. Had any of the salespeople at the store been at all helpful, I might have realized that, but they were just as clueless as I was.

I set out to find as much information as I could, and found a lot of conflicting information on the web. *What was I supposed to do with all that? I go to work and take Jack to his daycare. Would they work with me on this? Why don't more parents cloth diaper?*

That Saturday, I went back to the park and I asked some of the moms. Each one had a favorite brand and a diaper load of reasons to support their choice. But seeing the various diapers in action, and having some help was really great. Another dad was there this time too, and he had learned a few tricks that were very helpful.

Jack has been in cloth for eleven months, and now I'm in the group at the park that shares hints and tips. I've tried many different styles now, and I've come up with my top tips for dads.

Dads' Dirty Dozen

1. Don't even try to use safety pins. That's old school. My big hands are tough, but I poked so many holes in my fingers in a few days I can't even tell you. And the little spots of blood are the toughest things to get out! If you choose to use prefolded diapers, get some "Snappis" to fasten the diaper on or buy covers that hold them in place.

2. Find some all-in-one diapers. They fasten like disposables and you can adjust the legs and waist for a perfect fit. A perfect fit is the key to keeping those oozing messes contained inside the diaper. There are several brands and a million designs and patterns. But no pink for my boy.

3. Always use liners! That way you can dispose of the nasty, smelly gunk right down the toilet and you are left with just pee in the diaper (most of the time).

4. Use cloth wipes. They are easy to use and actually work a little better than those wimpy disposables. I just throw them right in the wash with the diapers.

5. Use a sprayer at the toilet to spray away solid poop before you put the dirty diapers in the diaper pail.

6. Do the laundry every other day if you can. Not only does it help you maintain your stash of diapers all the time, but my house never smells like dirty diapers at all. Use the detergents that the manufacturers recommend. They really get the stains out great.

7. Run the washer without anything in it once a week on the hottest cycle with a little bleach in it. I was creeped out about washing my own clothes in the washer at first, because I knew that little bits of poop had been floating around in there. I never actually saw any, but I knew they were there!

8. Find a daycare that will allow you to use cloth diapers. This took a little convincing, but after a week, the director of Jack's daycare said she would encourage other parents to use cloth too. I brought extra diapers in his bag every day, plus I brought an extra wet bag. I did compromise and allow them to use disposable wipes, but I brought in natural ones that I could live with.

9. Don't use diaper ointment unless you have to. Jack never gets diaper rash with cloth like he did when I used disposables, but I know that regular ointments will ruin the waterproof lining on the inside of the diapers. If your baby gets diaper rash, only use ointments that are approved by cloth diaper manufacturers.

10. Now about those changing tables in the men's room. Disgusting. I bring along a plastic pad to put down, and when possible, actually go to my car to change Jack. Then I can leave the dirty diaper in a wet bag in the car. I've been known to complete the one-handed diaper change when the alternative is putting my boy down on a dirty surface.

11. When it's warm out, Jack just wears his cloth diaper. That's as dressed as we men get sometimes. I'm getting him ready to just wear boxers.

12. Real men use cloth diapers. And we're proud of it.

There you go. That's your walk in my park. The park that smells sweet with flowers and grasses—and if there are any stinky odors wafting from the trash, I know they aren't from Jack's diapers. I have seen studies that say that cloth isn't much better for the environment than disposables. I personally choose to believe that cloth is much better, and I feel better knowing that Jack's poop won't be preserved in a plastic package for future generations to try to figure out what to do with it.

"I feel responsible — responsible with my money
and responsible with the earth's resources."

— *C.K., Virginia Beach, Virginia*

CHAPTER 9

AIRING DIRTY LAUNDRY:

HOW TO WASH YOUR CLOTH DIAPERS

Caring for your cloth diapers is quite easy if you use a modern brand that washes easily at home.

Although each manufacturer makes different suggestions in their washing instructions (and, yes, you should always follow the manufacturer's instructions in terms of washing cycles, water temperature, and recommended detergents), most will require similar steps.

Let's discuss the basic washing instructions so you know what to expect when washing your cloth diapers.

HOW TO HANDLE WET AND SOILED DIAPERS

Once your baby wets the diaper (just a little pee), you can simply put the diaper in a dry diaper pail until you're ready to do a load of laundry. A little more attention is required for poopy diapers. If the diaper requires pieces to be separated (like a pocket diaper requires the insert to come out), do so.

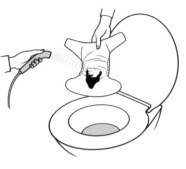

Knock off any loose solids in the toilet. (You are even supposed to do this for disposable diapers too!)

Spray off remaining solids with a Diaper Sprayer. (You can also use bio-degradable, flushable liners if you prefer not to use a sprayer.)

Toss dirty diaper into a diaper pail lined with a waterproof diaper pail liner.

Wash cloth diapers in approved cloth diaper friendly detergent and according to manufacturer's instructions.

Dry cloth diapers by line-drying or by drying on a medium dryer setting. (Do NOT use fabric softener sheets.)

STORING DIAPERS: HANGING DIAPER BAGS AND REUSABLE PAIL LINERS

Unlike cloth diapers of yesteryear that required soaking, swirling, and all sorts of other nasty storage solutions, you can simply store your soiled diapers until laundry day in an open hanging dry pail or reusable diaper pail liner.

Many moms store their diapers in a 42 liter/13-gallon-sized garbage pail with a lid (I like the ones with a foot lever lid). They line the pail with a reusable diaper liner that is washed along with the dirty diaper pile. Other moms like the hanging diaper pail that attaches to a doorknob or hook and simply hangs out in the open.

 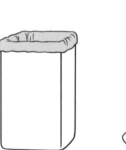 

The great thing is that you can wash the pail along with your diapers. FuzziBunz even makes a pail liner that has a zippered bottom so you can easily empty your dirty diapers into the laundry with little fuss.

Fluffy Stuff!

Some moms like to have two hanging pails: one in their baby's room and one in the bathroom. For easy (read that to mean *no poop*) diaper changes, you can put the soiled diaper in the pail in your baby's room. For hard (okay, the diaper contains poop) diaper changes, you can empty the poop into the toilet and then store the soiled diaper in a pail inside your bathroom. It's convenient to do it this way, especially after you've rinsed out a messy diaper with your diaper sprayer and don't want to drag it back into your baby's room.

For poopy diapers, knock any solids in the toilet. If it's a wet poo (from breast milk), you can usually just place it in the diaper pail and it will come clean when you wash it. Alternatively, you can rinse off the diaper with a diaper sprayer. It's a good idea to use a diaper sprayer for very soiled diapers.

DIAPER SPRAYERS

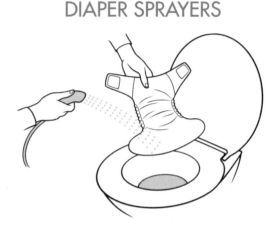

Diaper sprayers enable you to remove most (sometimes all) of the solids from the diaper right into your toilet, without having to use the dreaded dunking method. They attach directly to your toilet and work wonderfully in cleaning off those extra icky diapers.

The next step is to store the diaper in a dry diaper pail. There is no need to soak most modern cloth diaper brands. I recommend storing them no more than three days in a washable diaper pail bag or diaper pail liner. Just wash the bag along with the diapers—simple enough to do, right?

What Moms Say... about "diaper sprayers"

"After three months of cloth diapering I found out I was expecting again. My son was only eight months old and I just couldn't believe it! The morning sickness brought an interesting perspective to the stinky smell that also accompanied my son's new-found diet of solid foods. That's when I began to actually hate cloth diapering. I didn't own a diaper sprayer so I used an old rubber spatula to scoop the poop out of the diapers into the potty. It was disgusting!

"I cried and gagged every day for two weeks before my husband intervened and told me that I had to take a break from the cloth. I was so relieved! However, deep inside I felt like a failure because I had wanted it to work out so badly. I knew that cloth diapering was the right thing to do, but I just didn't want to deal with it.

"About a month later I broke down and purchased a diaper sprayer. All I have to say is the diaper sprayer has been a real home run! I pulled out all of the cloth diapers once again and gave it another go. Would you believe that is just what I needed and I have never looked back. For three months now I have really enjoyed cloth diapering again thanks to the diaper sprayer," says Julia W. from Suwanee, Georgia. ●

Fluffy Stuff!

For Mamas on the Go!

Inevitably your baby will soil a diaper when you're on the road. Take along a wet tote bag with you and simply store the soiled diaper in the bag until you get home. Then transfer the wet tote into your diaper pail until washing. If you're going to be away from home for a long time, you can opt to use a hybrid diaper, which offers a cloth insert or the option of an eco-friendly disposable insert.

DOING LAUNDRY

It is very critical to follow the manufacturer's washing instructions when caring for your baby's cloth diapers. That said, I recognize that most cloth diapering moms use several brands of cloth diapers and want to have the flexibility to wash them all at once.

 Here are some basic washing instructions that work for most cloth diaper brands.

☑ Empty soiled diapers from diaper pail into washing machine.

☑ Run a cold rinse to get rid of ickies.

☑ Add one-fourth cup of cloth diaper–approved detergent.

☑ Run a full hot water wash cycle.

☑ If needed, run a cold rinse cycle to get rid of leftover detergent.

☑ Line dry or tumble dry on low in your dryer.

Choosing the right detergent for your cloth diaper stash is important, and it can be a very personal choice too. I find that what works for one mom doesn't work for another based on water hardness, front versus top loading washing machines, and overall diaper brand they're working with. I also recommend sticking with one detergent. Mixing and matching detergents or switching your detergents can lead to residue or odor problems.

Whatever you do, make sure you use a detergent that doesn't cause soap scum buildup. Despite the label promise of being "free and clear," detergents with this claim tend to allow residue to build up that will eventually cause the diaper to repel moisture—just the opposite of the purpose of the diaper.

Also, use hot water for the longest cycle because you want to kill any bacteria. Just don't make it too hot (and don't use the sanitize cycle) or you may ruin the "waterproof-ness" of the outer shell. A cold rinse before and after the hot cycle ensures the diapers are extra clean and are best for really soiled or fuller loads.

Recommended Cloth Diaper–Approved Detergents

Here is a list of detergents considered to be safe for cloth diaper washing. Please be sure to check with the diaper manufacturer to ensure the brand you choose is safe for their diapers:

- Rockin' Green
- Allen's Naturally
- bumGenius Cloth Diaper Detergent
- Vaska
- Country Save
- Planet
- Lulu's In The Fluff
- EcoSprout

Check www.KellyWels.com for up-to-date listings on cloth diaper-approved detergents.

🌸 Fluffy Stuff!

Where can I buy recommended detergents, you ask?
Most cloth diaper retailers online offer cloth diaper–safe detergents. Many retailers also offer free shipping once you reach a particular dollar threshold.

Not Recommended

Here are some general types that are *not* recommended. Why? Because they may cause residue buildup that can lead to leaking or moisture-repelling issues. They may also cause premature wear and tear on your cloth diapers:

- Baby soaps
- Labeled as "free and clear" detergents
- "Natural" detergents
- Any detergent with fabric softeners, whiteners/brighteners, enzymes, fragrance, or bleach

OTHER WAYS TO CLEAN DIAPERS

Some common household products may be used to supplement the cleaning of your diapers:

Baking soda: 1 to 2 tablespoons of baking soda will help neutralize acid and odors. Baking soda can be used in place of detergent in the initial cold water wash, or substitute half of your detergent for baking soda in the initial cold water rinse.

Bleach: Although bleach is typically a cloth diapering "no-no," I do recommend a periodic bleaching of micro-terry inserts only—especially since micro-terry is prone to buildup and stink issues. Use about 1 to 2 tablespoons of bleach every few months. Just do not use it on other types of cloth diapers, especially those with PUL.

PLEASE NOTE: Some manufacturers explicitly state not to use any additives such as bleach or baking soda, and the use of these additives can void certain manufacturers' warranties. While every effort has been made to provide safe, reliable, and helpful information, I recommend testing these for yourself on one diaper to ensure it works fine for you.

Fluffy Stuff!

Here's an absolutely free way to rescue stained diapers without bleach. Line dry them. Even in the winter, you can hang your diapers on a clothesline outside or a drying rack, and the sun will naturally bleach them.

Most cloth diapers are safe for the dryer as well, although if you have a larger stash and don't need the diapers immediately, try hanging them (inside on a drying rack or outside) to dry and save energy.

"I feel like I accomplished something. Even when nothing else gets done, I know my baby will have a nice fresh, healthy diaper against his skin."
—D.D., Portland, Oregon

Fluffy Stuff!

If you are using a front loader, you can easily program your cloth diaper wash cycle. I set my machine on whites, pre-wash, extra-rinse, and heavily soiled. Every washing machine is different so just use common sense when selecting the cycles. Never set a cycle on sanitize, because it will be too hot for your diapers and can damage them.

HOW TO WASH WOOL COVERS

To wash wool covers, you'll need lanolin, a wool wash (Eucalan brand works well or you can use baby wash), and an empty jar to dissolve the lanolin.

Start by filling the sink with warm water (just enough to cover the wool fabric). Add a tad of wool wash. Gently massage the suds into the wool fabric. Let soak for five minutes. Drain sink and then fold the cover onto itself while squeezing the water out. Don't wring the wool because that will make it lose its shape. Then take a pea-sized amount of lanolin and put it in a jar, add hot tap water. This will melt the lanolin. Shake the jar until it's all dissolved.

Refill sink again with warm water and a tad of wool wash. Add the lanolin to the water too. Swish the water around. Turn wool inside out, put it into the water and gently work it into water. Drain and fold the wool while squishing water out of it.

To dry, lay the wool cover on a towel. Roll up the towel and squeeze the towel to help extract water from the wool. Then lay it on top of another towel and let air dry for twenty-four to forty-eight hours.

Fluffy Stuff!

Breathing New Life Into Cloth Diapers
Many cloth diaper manufacturer's offer elastic and Velcro-style replacement kits if your diapers are getting worn out. For a nominal fee you can receive these kits from an online retailer or direct from the manufacturer.

REMOVING ODORS

Most moms admit that odor is a problem once in a while when using cloth diapers. Most problems result from the bacteria buildup on the micro-terry and hemp inserts, which absorb moisture beautifully, but often retain the stench we desire to get rid of. Hard water residue also has been a stinky diaper culprit.

Here are some tips from real moms about how you can get rid of lingering diaper stink:

Strip the diapers and inserts. You may have heard the term "stripping your diapers/inserts." Basically, stripping means you first wash your diapers/inserts in very hot water without any detergent followed by a cold rinse cycle. Keep doing this until no bubbles or cloudy water remains.

Soak problematic diapers and inserts in the washer with a little detergent. Sometimes you need to let the detergent work its magic and it's not feasible to wash them over and over again. If this is the case, let the diapers soak in the washer for thirty minutes or even overnight with a tiny bit (about 2 tablespoons) of your favorite detergent. My preferred brand for getting out stink is Rockin' Green. After soaking, run them through the normal wash.

Rinse inserts after diaper changes. If you have a persistent stink problem, try rinsing out the inserts of your pocket diapers before tossing them in the diaper pail until washing. Leaving the urine in the inserts only invites the stink to stay and "marinate." A diaper sprayer can be useful in this situation as well.

Store diapers in open air. Contrary to popular belief, you don't need to seal off your diaper pail to prevent stink. In fact, the open air can help circulate the air around the dirty diapers between washings.

Wash more often. I was surprised to learn that some moms go as long as a week between washings! If stink is a constant problem, consider washing your diapers more often. If you're storing them for days and days between washing, then the stink is allowed to permeate the diapers and cause you problems in the long run. For best results, wash your diapers at least every two to three days.

Clothesline your diapers. Letting your diapers wave in the breeze and bask in the sun can make them smell as fresh as a newly bathed baby's bum. And they will last longer (without harsh drying cycles). Another tip: the sun naturally bleaches your diapers, so they'll be more stain-free.

Completely dry your diapers. Make sure your diapers and inserts are completely dry after washing them. If the inserts stay semi-damp and are stuffed into the diaper while damp, they can be prone to retaining odor.

Add water softeners if you have hard water or iron deposits in your water supply only. If you have hard water in your house, you'll need to add a non-precipitating water softener (such as Calgon or Spring Rain) to the initial hot wash and cold rinse. These water softeners suspend the residue and mineral deposits in the water and prevent them from being re-deposited on the diaper.

Try odor removers. Some manufacturers (like bumGenius) make odor removers that claim to eliminate odor-causing bacteria. These products are safe to use on most cloth diapers, but it's always important to go to the manufacturer's website to see what they recommend before doing so.

Remove bacteria. Are you wondering if the washer really gets out all the icky stuff when you wash them? Or if the fecal material will linger inside the washer and get into other clothes? Here's my answer: Washing machines are designed to remove all fecal material. However, if you're a little germophobic, run your wash cycle once or twice a month with no clothing and add bleach or a product called Bac-out to the wash cycle. Frankly, I've read research showing that your kitchen sink is dirtier than your toilet bowl or washing machine when it comes to germs.

CHAPTER 10

EXTRA STUFF YOU'LL NEED

Cloth diaper accessorizing is big business and full of confusing terminology and items that you may be unsure you'll even need.

WET TOTES AND WET BAGS

Wet totes (also called wet bags interchangeably) are great for storing soiled diapers when on the go because each holds about one (maybe two) cloth diapers and they usually snap or zip to keep messes contained until you get home. Once you get home, you simply shake the diaper out of the wet bag and then put both the soiled diaper and wet bag in the wash for laundering.

Fluffy Stuff!

For daycare use, purchase a wet bag that will hold six to eight diapers. The Planet Wise medium-sized wet bag fits six to eight diapers perfectly.

WIPES

Cloth wipes are a popular option for cloth diapering parents who want to make their entire diapering system reusable. The benefits of using cloth wipes are many.

One, they are convenient. You simply put the soiled wipes in the dirty diaper pail along with your soiled diapers and wash everything together. No separate fuss required!

Two, you save money because you never buy disposable wipes again. Most bowel movements can be easily cleaned up with two cloth wipes.

Three, you never throw anything away. Your entire diapering process involves zero waste. Now that's something to brag about for sure!

Remember, there are a variety of reusable wipes available on the market for you to choose from. Most are made from soft cotton or micro-terry fabrics.

To use, simply wet a wipe, wipe your baby's bum, then toss the used wipe in the diaper pail for laundering. No waste and your baby's bum will thank you for treating it with kindness.

For cloth wipes on the go, I recommend wetting ten Thirsties Fab Wipes under tap water. Fold them in half and stuff inside a Planet Wise small-sized wet bag. This is great for day trips.

SWIM DIAPERS

Most public pools require that babies wear swim diapers, and that's why the disposable diaper manufacturers knew they could make swim diapers disposable too. But there are reusable cloth options you can use as an alternative to the common disposable swim diaper.

Most public swimming pools require swim diapers that are not absorbent but that have the ability to contain solid waste. Nothing clears the baby pool faster than a "floater."

Normal cloth and disposable diapers will absorb tons of water and should not be used when swimming. They not only are worthless in absorbing urine when already soaked, but they can weigh down your poor baby as they absorb the entire swimming pool.

Reusable swim diapers have a waterproof outer cover, but the reason they work is that they have a mesh layer on the inside to keep solid waste contained. Check with your favorite cloth diaper manufacturers to find a swim diaper for your baby (keep two on hand).

Fluffy Stuff!

Swim diapers come with either plastic snaps or Velcro-style fasteners. Choose whichever you prefer. I prefer snaps because they are less likely to snag my baby's swimsuit and last longer in constant moisture.

CHAPTER 11

GOTCHA COVERED

Cloth diapering can be one of the most satisfying parts of new babyhood—both for your little one's bum and for your peace of mind, whether you choose to cloth diaper because of the environment or to save money or to just do it. In the end, cloth diapering makes sense.

You will have ongoing questions on your journey to becoming the ultimate Earth Mother. And where do you turn? Friends? Yes, if they're also cloth diapering. It's amazing the tips and tricks new moms share about lots of things such as breastfeeding, switching to solid foods, best places for the bargains on kiddie clothes, and, yes, cloth diapering.

The Internet? Yes. Seek answers to your questions on any number of unbiased, wonderful blogs and websites where you'll find a diaper load of information. Our virtual community is growing as fast as your toddler.

Sad may be the day when your cloth diapers are, figuratively, behind you. One day, you'll put away the diapers (for your next baby) and enter the days of successful potty training. But be happy in the sense that your baby has been through the early years with a soft fluffy bum.

I wish you well.

Fluffy Regards!

Kelly Wels

Sample, Simplify, and Save!

SAMPLE: To achieve success with modern cloth diapers, first be sure to sample many brands & styles before you make a large purchase.

SIMPLIFY: Once you find a brand you love, purchase that brand/style as the "main-stay" of your cloth diaper stash.

SAVE: Enjoy knowing that you will be saving over $2,000 versus using disposable diapers!

—*Kelly Wels*

CLOTH DIAPER RESOURCES

WEBSITES

The list of informational resources on cloth diapering is growing daily. For the most current list of resources and for places to buy cloth diapers and accessories, check www.KellyWels.com. Here are some great resources to get you started.

Diaper Jungle
www.DiaperJungle.com
A comprehensive resource for cloth diapering and natural living.

Diaper Pin
www.DiaperPin.com
An informational resource guide on everything cloth diapers. Forums, Cloth Diaper Retailer Directory, and Product Reviews are among the features.

Diaper Swappers
www.DiaperSwappers.com
A lively community that offers support to cloth diapering parents. A handy place to sell diapers that you don't need (or want).

BabyCenter (Cloth Diapering Group)

www.BabyCenter.com
An online resource dedicated to helping new parents make
informed decisions on everything parenting.

Cloth Diaper Finder

www.ClothDiaperFinder.com
Cloth Diaper Finder is a database that lets users pick and choose
the features they want in a diaper and have matches appear.

Mothering

www.Mothering.com
Online parenting community inspiring families to live naturally.
Philosophical and practical advice about family, because everyone
needs mothering.

BLOGS

Nowhere has it been more evident than the blogosphere that moms are loving—and writing about—their cloth diapers. The blogosphere is home to moms (and even a few dads too) sharing their cloth diapering journeys, hosting cloth diaper reviews, sharing stories (good and bad!) and offering advice and tips to anyone who'll watch their vlogs (video blogs) or read their content. Check www.KellyWels.com for the most current list of blog resources.

Go to the popular blogs dedicated to fluff (those sweet cloth diaper butts). I recommend these:

The Cloth Diaper Report
www.TheClothDiaperReport.com
The Cloth Diaper Report offers readers well-written, honest reviews of dozens of brands and styles of cloth diapers. Emi S. started the blog as a way to show her love of cloth diapering by offering detailed reviews and giveaways of cloth diapers and other natural parenting products.

The Cloth Diaper Whisperer

www.TheClothDiaperWhisperer.com

The Cloth Diaper Whisperer posts tons of information daily about a variety of cloth diaper brands, feature stories, tips and tricks, and contributions from members of the cloth diapering community.

Dirty Diaper Laundry

www.DirtyDiaperLaundry.com

Dirty Diaper Laundry offers a plethora of information about cloth diapers and regularly hosts giveaways (free diapers) and video reviews of various products. Kim R., the woman behind the blog, uses these products on her children and offers fair, unbiased reviews that inform parents who may be confused about cloth diapering and all the brands.

The Eco Chic

www.TheEcoChic.com

Calley P. started her blog writing about simple ways people could live a greener lifestyle. Once she started cloth diapering her baby, she focused on writing about her love of cloth diapers and promoting awareness through her strong social media presence.

KellyWels.com

www.KellyWels.com

I started my personal blog to educate parents on the ease and benefits of cloth diapering while offering parents opportunities to win free diapers. The blog also focuses on green living and networking with other mommy bloggers.

Other Great Blogs

www.AllAboutClothDiapers.com
www.ClothDiaperGeek.Blogspot.com
www.ClothDiaperBlog.com
www.ClothDiapers.Blogspot.com

TWITTER AND FACEBOOK

Just about every diaper company has embraced social media. Do a quick search for them and join their page. You'll be the first to hear about specials, news, and giveaways.

ORGANIZATIONS

Real Diaper Association
www.RealDiaperAssociation.org
A nonprofit organization that provides support and education to parents about reusable cloth diapers.

DECIPHERING
BRANDS

There are hundreds of cloth diaper brands for parents to choose from, but with choices come overwhelming feelings and anxiety. Knowing what is best for your family is up to you. Please allow me to help you understand your options and share with you a few facts about each of the most popular brands.

I am committed to remaining unbiased and offering only the facts of each brand. I do encourage you to do your own research because there are so many cloth diapering brands that just might be a great choice for you and your baby.

BabyKicks
www.BabyKicks.com
This company specializes in hemp diaper products and offers both fitted and pocket-style diapers, wipes, and inserts.

bumGenius
www.bumGenius.com
One of the most popular cloth diaper brands and the pioneer in the one-size diaper phenomenon. bumGenius offers one-size cloth diapers that use hook and loop or snap fasteners. bumGenius also makes reusable wipes, diaper sprayers, inserts, pail liners, odor remover sprays, and a variety of other diapering accessories.

Bummis

www.Bummis.com

Specializes in diaper service quality diaper covers (known as Super Whisper Wraps and Super Brites), washable fleece liners (good to use if you need to apply diaper cream and don't want to ruin the diaper), organic cotton prefolds, wet bags, and flushable liners. The Bummis cover has a top flap that serves to hold the prefold in place. The prefold then sits on top of the cover and then the cover fastens into place like a contoured disposable diaper. For added protection, you can use a Snappi to secure the prefold to the baby and then use the Bummis cover over the diaper to contain wetness.

Econobum

www.Econobum.com

A very simple one-size diapering system, making it an economical choice. You simply put the prefold inside the cover and fasten it to your baby with snaps. You can use a Snappi to hold the prefold in place for a more secure fit, and then use the Econobum as your diaper cover. You can wipe down the inside of the cover between uses.

Flip

www.FlipDiapers.com

Comes with an entire diapering system and options. You get the waterproof one-size cover, which uses a snap down system with three rises. It has a snap or Velcro closure too. The inside of the cover is made of a laminate PUL, so it can be wiped between uses. You simply lay the insert over the cover and fasten to your baby. The real options come with what insert you use. It can be an organic cotton prefold, a stay-dry micro fleece insert, or disposable inserts that look similar to a sanitary napkin.

FuzziBunz

www.FuzziBunz.com

The original pocket diaper was invented in 1999. This company started the modern cloth diaper revolution and is still very popular today. The diaper has a pocket opening and comes in sized diapers and a one-size option. Unlike the other one-size diapers where you size the diaper with snaps, FuzziBunz uses a sizing technique similar to adjustable waist pants, where you size the leg casings to get the best fit for your baby without the maze of snaps on the top front of the diapers.

gDiapers

www.gDiapers.com

Considered the first and leading hybrid diaper on the market. It's considered "hybrid" because it's half reusable/washable and half disposable. The disposable part looks similar to an oversized sanitary napkin and is made with very green materials and practices. It can be flushed down the toilet after swishing it around to break it up or disposed of in the trash. The company says the disposable pads will biodegrade quickly, even in an airtight landfill.

GroVia

www.Gro-Via.com

GroVia makes a one-size all-in-two diaper and comes in Velcro-style or snap fasteners. It comes with a waterproof outer shell that adjusts like a typical one-size diaper and has three rises. It comes with either reusable snap-in soakers (inserts) or disposable BioSoaker liners. The reusable soakers attach to the diaper's cover with a snap to secure it into place. They can be washed and used over and over again. The disposable and compostable BioSoakers look like sanitary napkins and are contoured with elastic around the edges. They also have a one-size all-in-one (AIO) diaper that snaps on the side of the diaper. Made for quick and easy changes.

Happy Heinys

www.HappyHeinys.com

Made with custom-milled fleece that comes in Velcro-style and snap style, as well as one-size and sized options. Their one-size diaper offers parents one of the most adjustable diapers in the industry with four size settings.

itti bitti

www.ittibitti.com

A unique cloth diaper designed in Australia. Their signature product, the Bitti Tutto, is a one-size cloth diaper with a no bulk design featuring a stay-dry suede-cloth inner and three bamboo/organic cotton soaker pads with color code snaps so absorbency can be customized.

Kissaluvs

www.Kissaluvs.com

Fitted one-size diapers that come in cotton fleece, organic cotton/hemp blend fabrics and are best known for its Marvels. This diaper requires a diaper cover. Their fitted diaper in size 0 has an umbilical cord notch to accommodate tiny newborns. Kissaluvs also makes a one-size all-in-one (AIO) option.

Knickernappies

www.Knickernappies.com

One-size pocket-style diapers that snap on the side (instead of snapping on the front like most diapers) and comes with two inserts. They also offer a wide range of diapering accessories including their top rated Super-Do Hemp Terry Inserts.

Mother-ease

www.Mother-ease.com

All-in-one (AIO) and fitted styles are made from terry cloth (they require diaper covers). I have found this brand to be a great nighttime diaper as the largest diaper size holds up to 15 ounces of fluids—and more when a diaper liner is used.

Rump•a•rooz

www.Rumparooz.com

One-size pocket-style diapers. The company's best known brands are called the Lil Joey diaper for newborns and the G2 one-size diapers with 6-r Soaker. The Lil Joeys have a snap down for umbilical cord care and can fill the gap before baby is ready for larger, one-size diapers.

Smartipants

www.Smartipants.com

One-size diaper with a pocket opening. The big difference is the design of the pocket and inserts: the system is designed for the insert to come out of the pocket in the wash (whereas with most pockets, the insert needs to come out before washing).

Thirsties

www.ThirstiesBaby.com

Makes fitted diapers, all-in-one style diapers, pocket diapers, and diaper covers with a Velcro-style or snap-style closure as well as a line of cloth diapering accessories. Made in the U.S.A.

For a complete listing of cloth diaper manufacturers, please visit *www.KellyWels.com, www.RealDiaperAssociation.org* or *www.RealDiaperIndustry.org.*

"Warm and fuzzy, Smart and green,
Cool and colorful."

—*F.C., State Line, Mississippi*

NOTES

"Diaper Debate: Cloth Makes a Comeback," CBC News, July 15, 2008, *www.cbc.ca/consumer/story/2008/05/16/f-consumer-disposablediapers.html.*

"Momprenuer, Owner of Kanga Care, LLC, Invents New Product That Proves Her Company Is Recession-proof!" *BabyShop Magazine,* March 23, 2010, *www.babyshopmagazine.com/ebs/2010/volume1/press-releases/rump-a-rooz.htm.*

"The Diaper Drama—Environment," The Diaper Pin, *www.diaperpin.com/clothdiapers/article_diaperdrama4.asp.*

U.S. Environmental Protection Agency, "Dioxin," *http://cfpub.epa.gov/ncea/CFM/nceaQFind.cfm?keyword=Dioxin.*

About.com, "How Diapers Work and Why They Leak," Anne Marie's Chemistry Blog, February 6, 2007, *http://chemistry.about.com/b/2007/02/06/how-diapers-work-why-they-leak.htm.*

Environmental Health Association of Nova Scotia, "Guide to Less Toxic Products," *www.lesstoxicguide.ca/index. asp?fetch=babycare#diape.*

Happy Heinys, "Linda Byerline, Founder Happy Heinys," *www. happyheinys.com/press_releases/presskit-bio.php?t=4.*

WebMD.com, "Solving Your Diaper Dilemma," July 27, 2008, *www.webmd.com/parenting/baby/diapering-a-baby-9/ diaper-choices?page=2.*

The Sierra Club, "Diaper Options: The Big Cloth-Versus-Disposable Debate," *www.sierraclubgreenhome.com/ uncategorized/green-diaper-options.*

Susan L. LeVan, "Life Cycle Assessment: Measuring Environmental Impact," Forest Products Society, June 1995, *www.fpl.fs.fed. us/documnts/pdf1998/levan98b.pdf.*

Pamela Paul, "Diapers Go Green," *Time*, Jan. 10, 2008, *www.time. com/time/printout/0,8816,1702357,00.html.*

ABOUT THE AUTHOR

Kelly Wels is a leading cloth diaper expert and advocate who has a passion for helping parents make informed decisions when it comes to how they diaper their babies.

In November 2010, Kelly founded *www.KellyWels.com*, which she calls her "passion project." Her mission is to share her love for cloth diapers and to advocate for diapering change. She says she believes that, through education and knowledge, parents can be empowered to make more positive diapering choices. Kelly also is a green living promoter and social media marketer.

Kelly was previously known by her peers as the founder and owner of *www.DiaperShops.com* and *www.KellysCloset.com*, two popular online cloth diapering stores. In the summer of 2010, Kelly decided to turn her business over to new owners and pursue her advocacy passion full-time, without dealing with the day-to-day pressures of running a multi-million-dollar business.

Most importantly, Kelly is mom to three children, Olivia, Hanz, and Riley.

got
cloth?

EXTRAS

PACKING THE FLUFFY CLOTH DIAPER BAG

Here is a list of suggested items to pack in a diaper bag for a day-trip outing:

- ☑ 6-8 cloth diapers (quantity is based on how often you are changing baby)

- ☑ 1 small wet bag (for cloth wipes, I recommend the Planet Wise wet bag small)

- ☑ 10 cloth wipes (fold in half, wet wipes, stuff inside small wet bag)

- ☑ 1 medium wet bag (for storing dirty diapers, I recommend the Planet Wise wet bag medium)

- ☑ 1-2 outfit changes

- ☑ 1 tube of cloth diaper safe cream (for example: CJ's BUTTer)

- ☑ 2 fleece liners (to be used if you apply cream to baby)

- ☑ 1 cloth changing pad (for example: FuzziBunz Changing Pad)

- ☑ Other baby and mama items as needed

FLUFFY GEAR

Use the following pages to help you keep organized. List the items that you have and what you need.

The following quantities are based on washing every other day. Increase quantities if you plan to go longer between washings.

ITEM	I HAVE	I NEED	RESOURCE (list store, URL, or other source)
18-24 cloth diapers			
6 diaper covers (only needed if using prefolds, flats, or fitted cloth diapers)			
36 cloth wipes			
1 roll flushable liners (100 sheets)			
2 pail liners			
3 wet bags			
1 diaper sprayer			
1 bag cloth diaper detergent			
6 fleece liners (to use if you need to apply diaper cream to baby)			
6 natural fibered doublers (or inserts) for nighttime use			
Other			

MY FLUFFY STASH

Here is a fun way to keep track of all your cloth diaper purchases!

Brand Name	Size	Style/Color/Print	Qty.	Place Purchased	Date Purchased	Price

MY FAVORITE FLUFFY STORES

Use these pages to keep track of your favorite cloth diaper retailers. For a listing of reputable cloth diaper retailers please visit *www.KellyWels.com, www.RealDiaperAssociation.org* or *www.RealDiaperIndustry.org.*

Store Name:	
Store URL:	
Facebook URL:	
Phone # / Address	
Items Carried:	
What I Like Best:	

Store Name:	
Store URL:	
Facebook URL:	
Phone # / Address	
Items Carried:	
What I Like Best:	

Store Name:	
Store URL:	
Facebook URL:	
Phone # / Address	
Items Carried:	
What I Like Best:	

Store Name:	
Store URL:	
Facebook URL:	
Phone # / Address	
Items Carried:	
What I Like Best:	

Store Name:	
Store URL:	
Facebook URL:	
Phone # / Address	
Items Carried:	
What I Like Best:	

MY FLUFFY THOUGHTS

INDEX

FASHION INDEX